WE WERE FREEDOM

return." I felt ever so sorry for my folks who would immediately receive a missing cable and then worry un... the next one arrived. But bad news will out so fasten. Naturally can't tell you events or circumstances concern... recent experience but might say "It was a long hard fight Pop, but I won." Ended up pretty slightly the worse for wear looking like a poplar tree in wintertime, weight 155 lbs. Not much meat on a frame like mine. But pommy-cart was the first read of glue, going to leave it on till I get to Cal. then go to a good hairdresser say "The works Kid." Leaving for Calcutta tomorrow for a Medical Board & sick leave. Sorry Shirl, had to break off and dash away. Here... one in Cal. Was quite sick at tummy for a few days but...

FOREWORD BY ANDREW COHEN
TEXT BY TIM COOK

WE WERE FREEDOM

CANADIAN STORIES OF THE SECOND WORLD WAR

A PROJECT OF THE HISTORICA-DOMINION INSTITUTE

KEY PORTER BOOKS

LIBRARY AND ARCHIVES CANADA CATALOGUING IN PUBLICATION

We were freedom : Canadian stories of the Second World War / Historica-Dominion Institute.

ISBN 978-1-55470-302-9

1. World War, 1939-1945--Personal narratives, Canadian.
I. Historica-Dominion Institute

D811.A2M455 2010   940.54'8171   C2010-901207-0

THE CANADA COUNCIL | LE CONSEIL DES ARTS
FOR THE ARTS | DU CANADA
SINCE 1957 | DEPUIS 1957

ONTARIO ARTS COUNCIL
CONSEIL DES ARTS DE L'ONTARIO

Canadian   Patrimoine
Heritage   canadien

The publisher gratefully acknowledges the support of the Canada Council for the Arts and the Ontario Arts Council for its publishing program. We acknowledge the support of the Government of Ontario through the Ontario Media Development Corporation's Ontario Book Initiative.

We acknowledge the financial support of the Government of Canada through the Canada Book Fund (CBF) for our publishing activities.

The Memory Project: Stories of the Second World War is made possible through generous funding from The Department of Canadian Heritage.

Key Porter Books Limited
Six Adelaide Street East, Tenth Floor
Toronto, Ontario
Canada M5C 1H6

www.keyporter.com

Text design and electronic formatting: Sonya V. Thursby, opushouse.ca

Printed and bound in Canada

10 11 12 13 14 5 4 3 2 1

This book is dedicated to the more than 1.1 million Canadians and Newfoundlanders who served in the Second World War and to the thousands of veterans who continued to serve by sharing their story of service and sacrifice through The Memory Project.

Lest we forget.

... bottom corner of the first page.

I felt ever so sorry for my folks who would immediately receive a "missing" cable and then worry until the next one arrived. But let well enough alone. Naturally can't tell you much as circumstances concerning recent experience but might say "It was a long hard fight too, but I won." Ended up finally slightly the worse for wear looking like a poplar tree in wintertime, weight 130 lbs. Not much meat on a frame like mine. But funny part was the fire beard I grew, going to leave it on till I get to Cal. then get a good hairdresser to say "The works kid." Leaving for Calcutta tomorrow for a Medical Board & sick leave.

Sorry Shirl, had to break off and dash away. Here I am in Cal. Was quite sick at tummy for a few days but

CONTENTS

...return. I felt ever so sorry for my folks who would immediately receive a missing cable and then worry until the next one arrived. But Oh well C'est da Guerre.

Naturally can't tell you events or circumstances concerning recent experiences but might say "It was a long hard fight (op), but I am." Ended up finally slightly the worse for wear looking like a poplar tree in wintertime, weight 135 lbs. Not much meat on a frame like mine. But funny part was the fine beard I grew, going to leave it on till I get to Eat then get a good hairdresser to say "the works old." Leaving for Calcutta tomorrow for a Medical Board & sick leave.

Sorry Shirl, had to break off and dash away. Was ... was ... Was quite sick at tummy for a few days but...

FOREWORD

Why remember? Why exhume the past? Why wander the corridors of memory, especially if they are dark, dank, long, narrow, and airless?

"The past," as the novelist William Faulkner memorably said of the American South, "is never dead. It's not even past." For Canada's veterans of the Second World War, this is particularly so. They returned home in 1945 and 1946 and resumed their lives in the postwar world they had created—studying, working, marrying, raising children. They were too busy, or too modest, to discuss the war.

It wasn't just the veterans who were silent but the war's victims, too. A generation of young Jews in North America, for example, did not really learn the horror of the Holocaust from those who had survived it until the 1970s. It wasn't discussed in polite conversation. If a memory is painful, our subconscious says, let it remain a memory. Let it rest.

And so it did. The Great War—in which Canadians fought and died in numbers unmatched in any conflict before or since—had been immortalized by a generation of poets and writers, including Rupert Brooke and Siegfried Sassoon in Britain, as well as John A. McCrae and Will Bird in Canada. By and large, though, the Second World War did not have that anguished afterlife. Veterans surely had a story, but they were reluctant to tell it. And truth be told, we were not eager to hear it.

By the 1980s, a generation removed from the great cataclysm, Canadians were losing interest in the military and in the Second World War, too. Few seemed to care what our soldiers, sailors, and airmen had done in that wasting season between 1939 and 1945. An unconscious country raised no memorial to those who landed and died at Juno Beach in 1944, for example, as a more reverential one had in France to those who died at Vimy Ridge in 1917. At eleven o'clock on Remembrance Day, we stopped pausing for a minute or two of reflection at school and work, as we had for decades. Fewer Canadians attended ceremonies at cenotaphs in towns and cities. Blame the zeitgeist.

That's changing in Canada today. In the last decade or so, there has been new interest, even affection, for our military, which has regained stature in public life. Surveys suggest that more people are turning out on November 11. Perhaps there is a greater understanding of the significance of the Second World War, popularized through film, television, and books, as well as in renewed institutions such as the Canadian War Museum in Ottawa. Perhaps it is because we are fighting in Afghanistan. As a country, it can be said, we are more curious about what happened across our oceans more than a half century ago. And those remaining veterans are more inclined to tell us.

Like any conflict, the Second World War has had its memoirists and chroniclers. In Canada, Farley Mowat has written poignantly of his experience as a young soldier in Italy. Meanwhile, J.L. Granatstein and David Bercuson are among the school of historians who have woven our wartime narrative. It is not that the veterans have not spoken at all. Many have. More likely, it is that most of the 1.1 million men and women who served in uniform have not told their story, either because they did not want to, or, more likely, because they were never asked.

We are asking. The Historica-Dominion Institute, an independent charitable organization dedicated to advancing memory and identity in Canada, is inviting veterans to remember. To this end, we have established The Memory Project: Stories of the Second World War. It is a two-year program to create the largest oral history of the Second World War in the country. Conceived by Marc Chalifoux and Jeremy Diamond, and led by Jenna Zuschlag Misener, the project has fielded a team of twenty-five researchers, interviewers, archivists, transcribers, translators, editors, and web designers. Although they are some two generations younger than the veterans they meet, their connection is often immediate and affecting. These men and woman travel the country seeking veterans to share their stories. We go to them—in private homes or retirement homes, in community halls, lodges, legions, and hospitals. We record, transcribe, and translate their stories. We photograph their medals and artifacts. Then we reproduce the interviews, digitize their memorabilia, and put them on their own website (www.thememoryproject.com), where all the interviews, in the words of veterans themselves, can be heard. Now, finally, we are preserving their recollections between the covers of a book. This is it.

Why now, sixty-five years after the end of the war? As The Memory Project Speakers' Bureau brought veterans into the country's classrooms to discuss the war—in ten years, these veterans have reached more than 1 million young Canadians—we realized that there would be fewer and fewer veterans to make these appearances. After all, the average age of a veteran of the Second World War is eighty-eight; they are passing away at a rate of four hundred to five hundred a week. Given this reality, it made sense to reach as many as we could as quickly as we could. With the generous support of the Celebrations and Commemorations Program of the Department of Canadian Heritage, The Memory Project: Stories of the Second World War was launched in the summer of 2009.

We have now interviewed some two thousand veterans, a number that will continue to grow in the last months of the project. It is important to note that ours is a national enterprise, conducted in both French and English (and sometimes other languages). In search of history, we are not bound by geography; we seek veterans everywhere, in all provinces and territories, in the deepest marches of Canada. And there we have found them—from the Yukon to Newfoundland to the places in between. They are black, white, and tan; Aboriginal and Asian; Punjabi and Polish, Christian and Jewish. They are Canada itself.

We Were Freedom: Canadian Stories of the Second World War is their testament. From our growing archive, we have selected the best of their accounts and divided them into five categories: service, connections, battle, home, survival. Given context by Tim Cook, an award-winning historian who wrote the introduction and the descriptive passages, and edited by Andrew Theobald, theirs is an intensely personal story. Here, in this catalogue as deep as the human psyche, you will find those terse, iconic elements of human conflict: blood, pain, dirt, cold, heat, joy, heart, soul.

Here is Murray T. Copot of Calgary, who served on a corvette in the Atlantic. His ship was sunk in the ocean and, as he struggled to swim to safety, he was driven by the desire to spare his mother an awful telegram announcing his death. At the same time that he was in the water, his mother stirred in the middle of the night, a world away, in Fraserwood, Manitoba. She woke her husband and declared with eerie intuition, "Something is happening to our son." Something was. They began to pray. Copot didn't talk about it for decades.

Here is Betty Dimock of Saint John, New Brunswick, who was a Canadian nurse in South Africa. It was her "great ambition" to serve in the war, and she did. But the reality of treating the Allied wounded transferred from the theatre in North Africa was shocking. Beyond imagination, really. There were often no antibiotics and few dressings in the rudimentary hospitals. "I needed a soup ladle to remove the pus and maggots," she recalls of one of the wounded.

Here is Mike Hawryliw of Fenwood, Saskatchewan, who volunteered to take part in the chemical tests at Experimental Station Suffield in Southern Alberta. He was one of hundreds who offered up himself for experimentation; they were given two days off for every week there, and that was appealing. Sworn to secrecy, paid twenty-four thousand dollars in compensation in 2003, Hawryliw didn't tell his family of the experiments for fifty years.

And here is Malcolm Andrade of Georgetown, British Guiana. He enlisted in the Royal Air Force in 1943. His role was to provide air support to armies in the field. One day he swooped in on a column of SS; seeing a lone dispatch rider running for his life, he "blew him apart." Later, on the ground, he encounters burning bodies. He still remembers the nauseating stench of death.

A happier memory: when the flyers returned to their bases, often in Holland, they would see kids on bicycles waving so enthusiastically to them that they would teeter and nearly fall off. "These little things get to you," remembers Andrade. "They saw the roundels on our aircraft and they said we were freedom, that's what we were."

We were freedom. Of course they were. For those in uniform in those siren years, that wasn't an empty conceit or idle boast. To the Normans in France or the burghers of the Netherlands and others in Occupied Europe, Canadians were saviours. They were tribunes of freedom, and, fundamentally, that was what the Second World War was about. It lacked the moral ambiguity of the Great War and Canada's other wars. To those who were there, the cause was so self-evident, so utterly indisputable, that there was simply no need to discuss it afterwards. We were freedom. In 2010, as the light fades and a generation dies, now is the time to declare it, record it, and celebrate it—with new gratitude and respect.

ANDREW COHEN
President, The Historica-Dominion Institute

INTRODUCTION

A WAR OF NECESSITY

Canada was never the same after the Second World War. The nation was wealthier, a recognized economic and military power, and more influential on the world stage. At home, birth rates boomed, education levels rose, the middle class prospered, cities expanded, and industry produced goods to modernize and create more time for leisure. Few would have predicted that the nearly bankrupt and disillusioned Canada of the Depression-plagued 1930s could ever achieve such leaps forward. But this enormous change was achieved on the backs of Canadians who served and sacrificed in the Second World War.

Canadians were at war from September 10, 1939, to the final surrender of Germany on May 8, 1945, and then until a few months later in August, when the already smouldering and shattered Japanese empire faced the terrifying atomic bombs that brought almost immediate surrender. While the Great War of an earlier generation had crawled to an end on November 11, 1918, the Second World War ended with the biggest bang in human history.

That is just one of the war's terrible legacies. The Second World War ushered in its wake the rise of new superpowers, the reduction of old empires, and the mixed legacy of decolonization. It also laid waste to populations, with some 50 million corpses encircling the globe. It allowed for the furthering of human rights in parts of the world, while other areas degenerated into unrest and slaughter. And soon the world was divided and under threat in the new Cold War, which had its birth in the dying embers of the Second World War. Few of these titanic events could have been foreseen by the generation that wearily turned to battle in 1939.

Throughout the late 1930s, Canadians had watched world events with growing concern and an increasing resignation that something would have to be done. Adolf Hitler's totalitarian regime in Germany had to be stopped, as did his international henchman Benito Mussolini in Italy and the military dictators in Japan. In the desperate attempt to avert war, European statesmen sought rational discourse, before giving in to self-delusion and the eventual sacrifice of small nations. Hitler thrived on Europe's weakness. He would not stop.

Few in Canada wanted war, especially after a Depression that had reduced millions to the indignity of swept-away farms and lost jobs. These grim times, combined with the grief-ridden memories of Canada's gut-wrenching losses of more than sixty-eight thousand dead in the Great War, left most Canadians supporting the British policy of appeasement toward Hitler. But after the Germans remilitarized, gobbled up Austria, made a second meal of Czechoslovakia (which had been served up by the panicking Western European nations), and finally invaded Poland on September 1, 1939, Canada was confronted by war.

Britain declared war on Germany on September 3, 1939. Canada did not. In August 1914 Canada was a colony within the British Empire, without control over its own foreign policy. When Britain went to war, Canada was automatically at war. Now, twenty-five years later, Canadians would decide its fate. At the helm of the nation was the waffling, unwarlike, and somewhat comical Prime Minister William Lyon Mackenzie King. The Canadian prime minister surprised many of his critics by guiding his country effectively through the difficult and divisive war—even though he always paled in comparison to the stately American president Franklin D. Roosevelt and the pugnacious bulldog of a British prime minister, Winston Churchill. But like his countrymen, King had steel running through him, and it showed.

While hundreds of thousands of Canadians felt the pull of Empire—the bonds of shared blood and history—there was no single reason why Canadians enlisted to fight so far from their shores. With Hitler's odious Thousand-Year Reich willing to make war on its neighbours, and perhaps the world, many saw this as Canada's war, a struggle that would eventually be brought to their own cities and families. Thanks to a flood of 1930s science-fiction stories and films depicting enemy bombers carrying high-explosive and chemical payloads, and touting the technical wonders of the ocean-crossing U-boats, Canadians no longer felt safe in their "fire-proof house." This was a war that had to be fought, a just war, and as the Nazi's systematic assault against civilian populations was revealed, many more Canadians felt it was their duty to make a sacrifice.

This just war, or Good War, as it is often described, forced Canadians to confront bestial evil. It required more than a million young men to go from their farms and factories to kill and maim, while fifty thousand women enlisted as nurses, and in the three services. It left families at home to wait and worry. It put sons and fathers, sisters and brothers, aunts and uncles in harm's way.

This Good War involved running the gauntlet of U-boats across the Atlantic in order to get the war-winning supplies from Canada and the United States to an isolated and increasingly vulnerable Britain. The Battle of the Atlantic, the longest running campaign of the war, claimed most of the 2,024 lives lost in the Royal Canadian Navy and the vast majority of more than 1,600 merchant seamen who died at sea. If that lifeline had been severed, as it looked like it might be when the U-boat wolf packs savaged the convoys in 1942, Britain would have been starved into submission, forced to sue for peace. "The only thing that ever really frightened me during the war was the U-boat peril," recounted Churchill. Canada's sailors did their part in ice-encrusted corvettes that were too often equipped with obsolete equipment, especially sonar (underwater echo-sounding). And still they sailed those rough waters; and still they refused to be driven into the safety of the harbours and the ports. By 1943, long-range aircraft, new tactics and technology, and more warships helped to turn the tide, eventually defeating the U-boats in the mid-Atlantic. By war's end, Canada's merchant navy

had expanded from thirty-seven ocean-going vessels to more than four hundred, while the Royal Canadian Navy was the third largest in the world.

Britain's difficult situation was all the more desperate after the fall of France in June 1940, and before the United States entered the war nearly a year and a half later. Britain expected a German invasion and it turned to its ranking Dominion for immediate support. Canada's land forces—first an infantry division, later joined by four more infantry and armoured divisions—were ready to defend Britain's shores. In the air, the outnumbered Royal Air Force (RAF) fought in the Battle of Britain to hold back the German fighters and bombers that sought to clear the way for a German invasion. More than one thousand Canadians served in the RAF during the battle, with the Royal Canadian Air Force (RCAF) also contributing No. 1 Squadron (later No. 401), which was equipped with Hurricane fighters in a death match against the Luftwaffe. With defeat staved off in October 1940 and Hitler forced to acknowledge that Britain could not be invaded, the Canadian army turned to training for a cross-channel invasion as the factories back home continued to churn out war-winning supplies for the Allied nations.

With the Canadian overseas army sitting inactive in the

United Kingdom and the Allies desperate to test the German defences, a series of raids was launched against the French coast, with the largest ordered against the town of Dieppe on August 19, 1942. It was a disaster, and a harsh warning that the German Wehrmacht meant to hold what it had snatched. Of a force of about 5,000 Canadians, 907 were killed, 1,946 were captured, and more than 2,400 were wounded. These losses were a stark reminder that success in returning to Europe through an amphibious landing would only come from thorough planning, a build up of amphibious vehicles and landing craft, and an overwhelming application of force. All the service arms would have to work together to get the infantry on the ground, and then to support them in defending against the counterattacks that would seek to drive them back into the ocean.

In other theatres of war, a doomed Canadian formation of almost 2,000 was sent to garrison Hong Kong against the Japanese. While most Canadians associate December 7, 1941, with the attack on Pearl Harbor—"a day that will live in infamy"—few are aware that on that same day two Canadian infantry battalions began their three-week struggle against hopeless odds in Hong Kong. After fierce battles against the Japanese, 290 Canadians were killed before the

surrender of the garrison force on Christmas Day. All of the survivors were driven into prisoner-of-war camps, where they were beaten, tortured, and starved. The war in the Far East continued: RCAF squadrons flew essential supplies to the forces in Burma, smaller groups of communication specialists processed intelligence in Australia, and Canadians served in British forces throughout the region.

In the summer of 1943, Canadians were a part of the Allied invasion of Sicily, with infantry, armour, and artillery driving through the island's rugged terrain, extreme heat, and malaria-infected regions. The fighting had been difficult during the thirty-eight-day campaign, with 2,200 casualties, but all expected worse to come on the Italian mainland. When the first forces landed in southern Italy in September 1943, there was little opposition. That did not last for long. Eventually 92,757 Canadians would serve in that theatre of war, advancing through the stunning beauty of the Italian landscape, clawing their way forward, attacking one ridge after another, with the Germans dug-in behind mine fields, barbed wire, and fire-swept kill zones. The so-called soft underbelly of the Axis Powers was anything but. Yet even with the defenders holding most of the advantages, with force-strength levels on par, and the enemy able to retreat from one prepared position to another, the Canadians blasted through the Germans in brutal combat. Still the Werhmacht dug in, holding shattered urban centres like Ortona, which the Canadians cleared in desperate house-to-house battles in December 1943. In May 1944, the Canadians crashed the feared Hitler Line and drove the Germans back in other butchering affairs. After the Normandy landings of June 1944, however, the supplies dried up and attention shifted to the central battlefield. The scarred veterans of Italy sneered, as only soldiers can about themselves, that they were the D-Day Dodgers—but their 24,885 casualties were stark evidence that they had dodged no fighting at all.

In order to strike back against Nazi Germany's war machine, open up a "Second Front" to relieve pressure on the Soviets, who bore the brunt of the enemy fighting forces from the summer of 1941, and raise sagging spirits and morale, the Allies turned to bombing German fortifications, transportation hubs, and cities. The British Commonwealth Air Training Program, which was established in Canada to train the air crews who manned the bombers, eventually produced more than 131,000 pilots, navigators, wireless operators, and gunners. It was not hyperbole when Roosevelt labelled Canada the "Aerodrome of Democracy."

Unleashing bombers against Germany was a grim way to wage war, but one of the few methods of striking directly at Germany. The enemy war machine was increasingly crippled, while schools and houses were also obliterated. Was there any other way? The occupied citizens of Europe, under the Nazi's crushing heel, would have said no. So too would the Jews and other targeted groups that were systematically rounded up, processed, and sent off to the death camps by the hundreds of thousands and then the mind-numbing millions—all of which was shockingly, and increasingly, revealed after the amphibious landings on D-Day on June 6, 1944.

With the full might of the Allied spearhead assisted by an enormous naval armada and hundreds of fighters and bombers—many from RCAF squadrons and the all-Canadian No. 6 Group in Bomber Command—the enemy fortifications and rail lines were pounded relentlessly. Behind the lines, Allied parachute formations dropped to disrupt enemy command and control capabilities, capture key installations, logistical hubs, and strong points. And on that Day of Days, five allied divisions, including the 3rd Canadian Division, landed on those fateful beaches. But as the Canadians drove inward from Juno Beach (their code-named landing site), the enemy did not fold. There were fierce battles against resolute German forces, including the nearly fanatical 12th SS Hitler Youth Division, made up largely of Hitler Youth teenagers and battle-hardened veterans from the Eastern Front.

The grim fighting throughout Normandy in the summer of 1944 proved that the enemy would hold on to the death. While the Allies had more artillery and command of the air, which allowed fighter bombers to bring down devastating rocket or cannon fire against soft-skinned vehicles, the Germans had better tanks and anti-tank guns, and had the advantage of fighting on the defensive on ground of their choosing. Any advance by the Allies brought horrendous casualties in the attritional fighting over farmer's fields and around small towns.

Front-line medics were the first in a chain of medical care that stabilized broken and shattered bodies, and moved the wounded from the fire zone through the system of surgery to care and ultimately back to the front, or to rehabilitation and discharge. Medical personnel also dealt with wounds to the mind. Accumulated stress, lack of sleep, and the constant wastage of comrades pushed many soldiers over the edge. Thousands fell victim to battle stress, the physical and mental breakdown that resulted from exhaustion and unending strain.

The defeat of the Germans in Normandy in late August did not end the war. After a brief pause, the Canadian Army was ordered to engage in a long struggle to clear the coastal towns, often with insufficient resources as the main Allied thrust shifted to the east. But the Canadians relentlessly pushed up the "long left flank," liberating city after city, and region upon region. The capture of Dieppe on September 1, 1944, brought grim satisfaction. But even in victory, the casualties were heavy and constant. There were no easy battles in the fall of 1944.

The Scheldt campaign of October 1944 seemed a shocking reprise of the flooded Passchendaele battlefield from 1917, with the Canadians scrambling in the muck and flooded polder fields as they brought to bear firepower from Lee-Enfield rifles, Bren guns, grenades, and mortars. The worn-out Canadians had a rest over the winter of 1944–45, but were back at it in the final months of the war, when II Canadian Corps liberated the Netherlands as the Dutch were on the verge of mass starvation, while I Canadian Corps (transported from Italy in early 1945) fought its way into the Rhineland, Germany. For the more than five thousand Canadians killed and wounded in the final months of the war as they ran up against a nearly fanatical German defence of soldiers and civilians, an end to the fighting seemed nowhere in sight. They welcomed the bombers that pounded relentlessly the German war machine and civilian centres.

At war's end, close to eight hundred thousand veterans moved from the military to civvy street, with another quarter million already demobilized, wounded, or killed. The transition could have been disastrous as veterans, mostly young men, flooded the job market. There had been unemployment and a sense of betrayal after the Great War, as veterans struggled to find their place in a debt-ridden society, but now the King government expertly managed the economy, transitioning from making "guns" back to making "butter." Perhaps most importantly, the passing of the Veterans Charter in 1945 was among the most forward-thinking legislation in the nation's history. Veterans were given loans to start new businesses or to build homes. As of early 1947, 33,828 veterans were studying in universities, which was almost the total number of university students before the war, in 1939. There were also payments for wounded veterans and their dependents. While many young men suffered with the lingering trauma of the war, afflicted with nightmares and depression, turning inwards or to the bottle for relief, most veterans moved on with their lives, eager to build up the country that they had helped to defend over the last six years. Some fifty thousand war brides settled in Canada and a baby boom was the surest sign of the prosperous and exciting times ahead.

In the end, few on the Allied side would contest that this world war was a war for good, but perhaps it was not a Good War. With more than forty-seven thousand Canadian wartime dead and another fifty-five thousand wounded, the shock of battle ensured that even in triumph, there was terrible grief, anger, and emptiness. But if it was not a Good War, perhaps it was a War of Necessity, with necessity demanding that almost any burden be shouldered, any cost born, any opposition broken. Victory was achieved, but the sacrifice was enormous and far reaching. Canada would never be the same.

TIM COOK

BATTLE

A few hours of battle might define a soldier's entire war.

Before battle, each and every combatant stood on his possible execution day. How to respond? How to go forward? Training helped, so did inspiring leadership and careful preparation, but every man knew that in a few hours or a few minutes, it might be over. Or worse. Death could be accepted, but maiming was too horrible to contemplate. How would a twenty-five-year-old go through life with one arm, or blinded, or hideously burned? The mind played cruel tricks.

No one reacted to pressure in the same way. Anxiety gnawed and nibbled, forcing some men to talk constantly in order to relieve their stress, while others turned inward, finding solace in silence. Bladders felt full, even after constant relief; food was refused for fear of a gut wound that would go septic more quickly. Humming a song; rereading a lover's letter; clutching a talisman; getting in a final game of poker. Warriors told themselves they would not get it. Some would die today, but not them. Others embraced the fatalism. If their number was pulled, it was all ordained by fate, God, or something else—so what was the worry? There was no single ritual accepted by all men, although all had some sort of ritual.

At some point the waiting ended. Moving forward from a slit trench, flying over a target, dropping depth charges in the hope of shattering the hull of a submerged U-boat: this was battle. Direct action assuaged much of the stress. Having a chance to close with the enemy—while often more dangerous than the waiting period—allowed for activity, action, and agency.

The brutality of combat deadened the senses through unremitting assault. The cacophony of anti-aircraft fire or high explosives created a physical sensation, a blanket that enveloped men. The different weapons of war intermingled and coalesced with the rising and falling screams of the maimed, creating a weird banshee wail.

Something wicked was looming. Sight was curtailed

102 ON ROLL   34 WOUNDED 24 DIED

73

NOMINAL ROLL and CASUALTY LIST OF "C" COMPANY, AUGUST 19, 1942. AT DIEPPE.

MAJOR. GREEN	COY. H.Q.	
CAPT. ELLIOTT	14 PLATOON	WOUNDED
" HOUGH	15 "	
LIEUT. GREEN	13 "	DIED OF WOUNDS
SGT. LENNOX, A.	14 "	
" LEOPOLD, J.	15 "	WOUNDED
L/SGT. GAMBRIEL, H.	13 "	"
SGT. SNOOK, M.Y.	COY. H.Q.	
CPL. ARNOTT, P.	13 PLATOON	
" BRUCE, G.	COY. H.Q. (S.B.)	WOUNDED
" GRONDIN, H.	13 PLATOON (H.Q. COY.)	
" MACKO, F.	15 "	
" MacDONALD, H.	15 "	DIED OF WOUNDS.
" O'REILLY, J.	14 "	WOUNDED
" SAKER, L.	15 "	"
" SCHARFE, H.	14 "	"
" SHEPHERD, C.	13 "	"
" SNYDER, L.	14 "	
" STEVENSON, C.	13 "	
L/CPL. DONNELLY	13 "	DIED OF WOUNDS
" GORMAN	COY. H.Q. (SIG. SECT. H.Q.)	WOUNDED
" LOOMIS, L.	14 PLATOON	"
" McMILLAN	15 "	WOUNDED REP
" PERCY, K.	13 "	
PTE. AHERN	15 "	
" BOULTINGHOUSE	13 "	DIED? MISSING IN UNITB
" BRADLEY	COY. H.Q. (SIG. SECT. H.Q.)	
" BUNYAN	14 PLATOON	
" CLOUTIER, M.	13 "	DIED OF WOUNDS
" CHASE	16 "	WOUNDED
" COLE, G.	13 "	WOUNDED
" COLE, J.	13 "	
" CORMIER, A.	15 "	DIED OF WOUNDS
" COYLE, M.	14 "	
" CRAWFORD, C.	15 "	

STANDARD TIME

1 BD J NL GB 2 extra.

Ottawa, Ont. December 26-44

William B Sturgeon, Report Delivery,
No 1 Noyan, Que.

24720 Minister of National Defense deeply regrets to inform you that D 144618 private Neil Mosser Sturgeon has been officially reported missing in action thirteenth December 1944 stop. When further information becomes available it will be forwarded as soon as received stop To prevent possible aid to our enemies do not divulge that of casualty or name of unit.

932a   Director of Records

37RMC 80 2 EX NL GB RELAY

OTTAWA ONT MAR 7-45

MRS MARGARET FORBES
REPORT DELIVERY
1438 PILLETTE RD WALKERVILLE

FOR PROMPT SERVICE—CALL 3-2476 and 3-2477
DEVONSHIRE AT ASSUMPTION
WALKERVILLE, ONT.

50666 SINCERELY REGRET INFORM YOU A54654 PRIVATE JOHN RAMSAY DOUGLAS FORBES HAS BEEN OFFICIALLY REPORTED SLIGHTLY WOUNDED IN ACTION FOURTH MARCH 1945 NATURE OF WOUNDS NOT YET AVAILABLE STOP WHEN FURTHER INFORMATION BECOMES AVAILABLE IT WILL BE FORWARDED AS SOON AS RECEIVED STOP WHEN ADDRESSING MAIL ADD WORDS IN HOSPITAL IN BOLD LETTERS OVER NAME OF ADDRESSEE FOR QUICK DELIVERY STOP TO PREVENT POSSIBLE AID TO OUR ENEMIES DO NOT DIVULGE DATE OF CASUALTY OR NAME OF UNIT

DIRECTOR OF RECORDS

or clouded entirely. Smoke and dust covered the battle-field. Tanks charged into the murk, unsure of what was in front or to the flanks. Ships operated under the ghostly glow of flares, sailors desperately scanning the water for the outline of an enemy U-boat in the green-tinged twilight glow. The olfactory senses were assaulted too. The smell of cordite mixed with freshly spilled blood and the pungent aroma of axel grease; these and countless other smells imprinted on the mind, and later memory.

Combat was a hammer dropping. It reverberated. It displaced. It shattered.

Those in battle talked about the experience like a film, but with sequences out of place. Perhaps it was closer to snap shots. Some things were remembered: the flash of a rifle muzzle, blood sprayed over a cockpit, fire raging through a Sherman tank, or the calmness of the ocean cut by a torpedo. The strangeness of battle was almost impossible to convey. It was at once dreamlike and nightmarish.

The aftermath was a time of exhaustion, shock, and grief. Comrades and crew lay among the contorted dead. The wounded writhed in agony, waiting for relief and transport to the rear. Enemy combatants, now prisoners, were studied curiously, often revealing the frightened and filthy, rather than the Nazi supermen of posters and propaganda. With the dead on both sides buried, combatants had to deal with the private battle of having killed. For some, it was easy to rationalize; others found the role of executioner hard to square with who they were. Such thoughts were often pushed from the mind in the moment, although they could creep back in—days, months, or years later.

Left: Nominal roll and casualty list from "C" Company, The Essex Scottish Regiment, following the Dieppe attack of August 19, 1942.

Top right: Telegram reporting Neil Mosher Sturgeon missing in action, December 26, 1944.

Bottom right: Telegram reporting that Private John Forbes has been wounded, March 7, 1945.

George MacDonell

BORN » EDMONTON, ALBERTA
BRANCH » THE ROYAL RIFLES OF CANADA, CANADIAN ARMY
TRADE » NON-COMMISSIONED OFFICER
HOMETOWN » TORONTO, ONTARIO

George MacDonell's experience contradicts the perceived wisdom about the Battle of Hong Kong, the Canadian Army's first combat engagement of the Second World War. After completing intensive training and rising to become a sergeant (and later a company sergeant major), MacDonell joined the Royal Rifles of Canada for their fateful trip across the Pacific. In vicious fighting with the Japanese invaders over seventeen days in December 1941, the Canadians were ordered to surrender. Nearly three years of suffering in Japanese prison camps and slave-labour gangs followed, but the Canadians always resisted.

After training at Wolseley Barracks, I went to the Royal Rifles of Canada, which had just been mobilized and needed weapons instructors. I served in that regiment until it was nominated in the fall of 1941 to proceed immediately to Hong Kong.

Within a month or so, the Japanese attacked Hong Kong in overwhelming force; their navy, air force, and a massive army. Within three weeks, the island was overrun and the governor was forced to surrender.

Then began almost four years in Japanese prison camps. I spent the first year or so in Hong Kong and then I was shipped to Japan. We were in Yokohama, in a place called Camp 3B, working in Japan's largest shipyard building Japanese freighters and naval vessels. In order to strike back at the Japanese, two young men—Staff Sergeant Clarke and Private Cameron—decided that they would commit sabotage through arson, damage the shipyard so that it could not produce the ships it was scheduled to complete. They started a fire that was timed to occur when the prisoners were back at their camp, about two miles away, during the night. The fire was set under the blueprint factory and the place where the wooden forms are patterned—the pattern shop. Since in those days there was no electronic storage of information, once you burned the blueprints and the patterns, there was no way you could build a ship or do anything in that shipyard.

The shipyard employed thousands of people. It was the most vital Japanese war effort, and it was destroyed by two young Canadians. They did it in utter secrecy—they told no one—but they pulled it off successfully and they even saved their own lives by doing so undetected.

> *"The story...is not about how the Canadians were defeated. It's about how they fought and how they behaved against impossible odds."*

After Yokohama, we were moved to a camp in northern Japan called Ohashi and were working in a mine when the emperor of Japan surrendered to the Allied forces. The Japanese army was furious at this surrender and, in fact, revolted. They tried to capture the emperor and continue the war, but they failed. We were left in a very dangerous position, surrounded by hostile Japanese troops, without any arms and so badly starved that we were in the last ex-

tremes of starvation and one form of illness after another. We were fed by air after a week or so, when the American forces spotted our camp. It took almost a month for the Americans to assemble the appropriate forces to a nearby port to pick us up.

The story, however, is not about how the Canadians were defeated. It's about how they fought and how they behaved against impossible odds. And it's about the mettle they showed when it was apparent that there was no hope and no possibility of a successful outcome. They never surrendered and they fought like tigers.

Left: Liberation Day, Ohashi Prison Camp, Japan. September 15, 1945.
Right: MacDonell in Tokyo, Japan, July 7, 1943 (right), and on August 5, 1941 (left).

Ernest Peter Bone

BORN » DEPTFORD, ENGLAND
BRANCH » NO. 626 SQUADRON, ROYAL AIR FORCE
TRADE » AIR GUNNER
HOMETOWN » VANCOUVER, BRITISH COLUMBIA

In June 1943, Peter Bone arrived in Canada from England as part of the British Commonwealth Air Training Plan. At the time, all he knew about Canada was "the Fraser River and its salmon and the Rockies," and that it was "darn cold." As an air gunner, he and his Bomber Command crewmates conducted twenty-five sorties against Germany and German-occupied Europe throughout 1944–45.

As a navigator in training, I used to fly around and around Winnipeg by day and by night. At night, we always knew where we were because we could see Winnipeg like a twinkling pincushion in the distance through the mist. It was always in sight. But we flew round and round it. Our pilots were not smart, uniformed air force pilots. They were former bush pilots and they used to wear lumberjack shirts and baseball caps, and they used to smoke the most horrible smelling mini cigars in the cockpit. They were bored silly, of course, training us.

We had to give them the ETA (estimated time of arrival) of a place ahead on our route. And that was my downfall, I'm afraid. I just wasn't quick enough—I wasn't fast enough in my thinking in the air. Generally, I would hand up my little piece of paper to the pilot and he would look at me and then take his cigar out of his mouth and growl at me and say, "We passed Carberry ten minutes ago, bub."

After a little friendly chat with the chief instructor, I was chucked off the course and sent to the Brandon [Manitoba] holding unit, where all failed air crew people were re-mustered to other air crew trades. The bomb-aimer course was nine months' wait and they weren't going to let me sit around peeling potatoes for eight, nine months, so they made me an air gunner.

There's been a lot of controversy that we should have adhered to the Geneva Convention, of which Britain, of course—and Canada, I suppose—was a signatory in the mid-twenties, when bombing was purely theoretical. There were no wars on. I've wrestled with this over sixty years and I've heard all the criticisms and the arguments

and so on, but I honestly believe that if we had adhered to the Geneva Convention it would have meant that we just didn't bomb German cities. Because all their armament manufacturing was in the big cities, and around the big cities, around the factories, were the workers' homes. It was inevitable that by bombing the German factories, we would also be bombing the German people, factory workers' homes, and all their ancillary installations—just as in Britain, just like the *Luftwaffe* in their bombing of British cities. We knew damn well that there was tremendous collateral damage.

And of course, Hitler could only send over two hundred aircraft at the most every night during the Blitz, because that's all he had. By the time we were operating, we could drop ten times the amount of tonnage on German cities that they dropped on us. And a lot of people have said to me, well, you should have dropped on the

Left: Bone with his Lancaster crew, just after VE-Day.
Right: Bone cleaning the Perspex turret on his Lancaster.

German cities what they dropped on you, as though war was a hockey match—the two sides have to be even and there has to be a referee, and people are sent off if there are penalties—forgetting that war, especially the Second World War, was a life-or-death matter of survival. It was either them or us.

"Sometimes the only way to overcome a great evil is to resort to a lesser evil."

Sometimes the only way to overcome a great evil is to resort to a lesser evil. There is no black or white in war, only gradations with much grey in between. It isn't a simple matter of idealism; there's no morality in war. It's useless to look for morality in war because war isn't moral. War is evil, and killing people is evil. But there are times when it has to be done and Britain and the Allies, or Britain, particularly under Churchill, wasn't prepared to take that awful risk to adhere to the Geneva Convention.

Fraser Muir

BORN » WESTVILLE, NOVA SCOTIA
BRANCH » NO. 50 SQUADRON, ROYAL AIR FORCE
TRADE » MID-UPPER GUNNER
HOMETOWN » WASAGA BEACH, ONTARIO

Hailing from the mining town of Westville, Nova Scotia, Fraser Muir of No. 50 Squadron vividly recollects the "two scary parts of an operation" with Bomber Command: taking off while carrying thousands of pounds of explosives and dropping those same explosives over the flak-filled skies of Germany. A mid-upper gunner, Muir completed thirty-five such operations in 1944–45.

I joined the air force because being the weight of 135 or 140 pounds, the army was not even being considered. The navy...I had no great love for the ocean, so the air force was always my choice. I joined in Halifax when I was eighteen.

When our postings were put up on the board, I was devastated. Al LeBlanc and Johnnie McKlay and Mel Orr were sent to Six Group, which was the Canadian group and, lo and behold, I was sent to Five Group. Now, as I say, I was literally devastated. I couldn't believe that I was all by my lonesome, heading for Five Group and the three of them were together, going to Six Group. The irony of it all was that I was the only one that came back.

Five Group was a so-called special group. Bomber Command would go out, eight hundred of them, and then you'd see in the paper the next day that Berlin was bombed by eight hundred aircraft Bomber Command. And then, down in the small print, you would see two hundred aircraft bombed an oil refinery or a bridge or a dam or submarine pens. Well, that was us. We did most of our trips with two hundred, 225 aircraft.

There were two scary parts of an operation. The first was the takeoff—whether or not we were going to get off the ground with a full load of bombs and gas. We'd go down the runway, everybody waving, one hundred or so people lining the runways to give you the thumbs up. The aircraft would be shaking and you're wondering if you're going to get off or not. Then you'd realize, once you got up one hundred feet or so, that you were okay, and then it would be complete silence, and just a beautiful feeling of relief.

Muir's Crew, 1944. Muir is bottom left. Top: John Broscoe, bomb aimer; Ken Thompson, wireless operator; Kenny Parkinson, engineer; Jack Paine, navigator. Bottom: Fraser Muir, mid-upper gunner; Tommy Groves, pilot; Blair McSwane, tail gunner.

"Mother of God, it was aircraft going up, crossing over in front of you, above you, below you."

I used to say that being in the turret at the end of the aircraft, you don't see anybody else. The five guys up front see each other, so they had that company. But back in the tail, in the turret, I was sitting on sort of a canvas sling seat and I used to say it was the coldest, loneliest place in the world. The duty of an air gunner wasn't to say shoot down other aircraft—we were the eyes of the crew. We couldn't for a second stop searching the skies for enemy aircraft, but also our own. We just flew out and we had no formation flying. We just took off and there was two hundred other aircraft up there, doing the same thing as you're doing.

Mother of God, it was aircraft going up, crossing over in front of you, above you, below you. And so the gunners had to warn the pilot if there was any other aircraft, no matter if they were enemy or friendly. My most vivid memories are of the planes above you. You're looking up—I can still see it in my dreams—there's an aircraft above us, doing the same thing as our aircraft, trying to line up the target with flares. And he's got his bomb bay open and you're staring there with fourteen one-thousand-

Muir (left) and Johnny Broscoe (right), autumn 1944.

pounders, or hundreds and hundreds of incendiaries and one huge four-thousand-pounder. And I'm screaming. He's right above us, he's going to drop, he's doing the same and here's the pilot and the bomb aimer trying to concentrate and line up. And they're yelling for me to shut up. And then the pilot would order me, "Pull your plug out for God's sake! Shut up," he would say. And so the guys would give me shit afterwards, you know, "you're so goddamned loud, Muir." But that's the way it was.

The longest and scariest time, I'm telling you, was after the bombs were gone. We had to stay straight and level because a couple of seconds after the bombs dropped, the flare went down and if you were at the right height, and everything was in line, the photo flash would go off when the bombs hit and the camera in the aircraft would take the picture. And the bomb aimer would be counting one thousand, two thousand, and I'd be screaming to count faster. The bomb aimer would say that's it, and the skipper would peel off and we'd be on our way home. But it was always a scary moment, and one that I'll remember to my dying day.

Jim Peters

BORN » MOOSE JAW, SASKATCHEWAN

BRANCH » HMCS REGINA AND HMCS ONTARIO, ROYAL CANADIAN NAVY

TRADE » LEADING DEPTH CHARGE OPERATOR

HOMETOWN » BAIE-D'URFÉ, QUEBEC

After joining the navy in February 1942, Jim Peters "went aboard HMCS *Regina* and...spent the next four years bouncing around from ship to ship." That bouncing around sent him to many parts of the world, including the Soviet Arctic port of Murmansk and the Red Sea. On February 8, 1943, Peters was at depth charge action stations in the *Regina* when she sank the Italian submarine *Avorio* off the coast of Algeria.

The day after I was eighteen, I was down at the barracks in Montreal. And within a week, I was down in *Cornwallis*, in Nova Scotia—it's the name of the barracks down there [near Digby, Nova Scotia].

I met a guy in the hall, he was crying. Me, I'd been looking forward to being there. I wasn't crying. I said, "What's the matter?" He says, "I got this ticket." And I said, "What do you mean, ticket?" He says, "Well, I have to go aboard HMCS *Regina* tomorrow." I said, "Well, do you want to change tickets?" He said, "Yeah!" So we changed tickets.

I went aboard HMCS *Regina* and I spent the next four years bouncing around from ship to ship. All in all, I was on board four different ships. Someone would always ask for a volunteer and I was always there. Other than my time with my family, they were the best four years of my life. I became a man and I loved it.

We sank a submarine during the course of one fight. We took aboard twenty-six Italian prisoners. The ones that were left alive when the submarine popped up to the surface all jumped in the water. We picked up as many as we could, and took them into shore in North Africa.

I was starboard lookout on the upper bridge—strapped in. I look up ahead and I see this wall of water coming at us. It turned out to be a sixty-foot rogue wave and I was up to my chest in water. And then the ship shook like mad and worked her way out of it; it's like going up a hill. But all the windows in the deck below, which was the steering room, it wiped out all the windows—wiped out all the Carley floats [inflatable life rafts] and the one lifeboat.

I was in charge of the after rail, which held the depth charges. They would call down, "set the depth for fifty feet." So you'd turn a little knob on the depth charge and then you'd hear, "roll one on the right rail" or the starboard rail. So we'd pull the handle and we'd go, "roll two." You set the depth and hope—cross your fingers that it worked. And that's what got the submarine.

So they were saying we were going to go into the Pacific theatre of war, but we were down at the foot of the Red Sea on the cruiser and they turned on all the lights at night. We had never seen lights for four years at night. And they said "the Japanese have surrendered, the war is over." And they lit up the whole ship. That was quite a sensation. I wondered if maybe there was a stray submarine that hadn't got the message yet.

Above: Italian prisoners from the submarine *Avorio*, sunk by HMCS *Regina* in 1943.
Top right: Montreal, 1942. Peters is in the bottom row, third from the left.
Bottom right: HMCS *Regina*.

Jan de Vries

BORN » LEEUWARDEN, THE NETHERLANDS

BRANCH » 1ST CANADIAN PARACHUTE BATTALION, CANADIAN ARMY

TRADE » PARATROOPER

HOMETOWN » PICKERING, ONTARIO

34

During the Second World War, Jan de Vries, who came to Canada from The Netherlands as a child, helped to liberate the country of his birth while serving with the 1st Canadian Parachute Battalion. He and his comrades saw some of the hardest fighting of the war, including being dropped into Normandy in the early morning of June 6, 1944, the Battle of the Bulge, and the Rhineland campaign.

I was born in Holland in the city called Leeuwarden and I came here in 1930 as a six-year-old. When I arrived, my dad said, you're in Canada now, be Canadian. And that's what I became.

I went to Bulford, England, and Salisbury Plain. All of the unqualified paras were immediately sent to Ringway, England [Royal Air Force parachute-training facility, near Manchester], where we were processed and had to do three balloon jumps—two in the daytime, one at night—and then five out of an aircraft with a hole in the bottom. If you didn't arch your back and clear the chute, you'd tip forward and ring the bell on the far side of the hole. We had lots of bleeding noses and broken noses in those days.

I managed to arch and clear, but the first jump was quite a thrill. You drop about 180, 200 feet and then you hear a nice quiet rustling. We didn't learn until afterwards that you don't have the prop blast or a plane flying one hundred miles an hour to help open your chute; it's just the speed of your falling body that opens the chute. That's why it took so long. Anyway, I got heck for not paying attention. I was so happy when the chute opened; I just decided to look around the countryside. Nevermind the instructions coming from the ground.

When I arrived overseas, I had never fired a gun. So when I went on the ranges and they looked at my target, they said, you'd better take a Sten gun [lightweight submachine gun] and spray them. They figured I couldn't fire a gun accurately enough. I became a bombardier and I went in on D-Day with the Sten gun, seven spare [magazines]

in a bandolier, a two-inch mortar with six mortar bombs in a container, all kinds of grenades. That was my job. If the enemy got close, I was to take them out with either grenades or the Sten gun.

On June 5, we went back to the planes in Harwell [a Royal Air Force base in Berkshire, England]. These were Albemarle bombers and they had a hole the size of a bathtub, not like the three-foot diameter ones in the Whitleys. We used to like that. We flew over and it was a quiet run. Nobody did much speaking. When we got to the French coast, the Ack-Ack [anti-aircraft fire] came up and we could see the lights of the flashing explosions and whatnot. Anyway, the pilot got nervous and he took evasive action, like most of the pilots did. They were all green, like we were.

We were going down on top of Germans who had been in war for five years; we'd never been in a battle yet. The pilot got lost in the drop zone. He got rid of us by putting

Right: Battledress worn by de Vries during the war.

on the light. I landed on a field. I had no idea where it was. We were so slow getting untangled and getting out of the aircraft. But I remember one guy who sat at the other end of the hole with a Bangalore torpedo around his neck, he got made a POW and he died in Czechoslovakia. The Germans shot him for some reason.

The Ardennes came up in Belgium, the Battle of the Bulge, and we were a ready-made division. On Christmas day, we went into Belgium and eventually Rochefort and Roy and then Bande. Now, Bande was a place where the Germans had shot thirty-five young Belgians in retribution for something—shot them in the back of the head and threw them in this basement. I've been back there since and put a plaque up there.

After that, we went to Holland to relieve a division. We were across the river from the Germans at Roermond. Eventually, I think it was in February [1945], we went back to England to be reinforced. We regrouped, and dropped over the Rhine River into Germany. Now, that was a lot

"The field was covered with guys who had been killed or wounded. I heard bullets going by and I looked up and my chute was full of holes."

different than the night drop in France. This was ten in the morning, on a bright sunny day. The Germans were waiting for us and they opened up on us as we were coming out of the aircraft. They shot down about thirty aircraft and got a lot of our fellows. The field was covered with guys who had been killed or wounded. I heard bullets going by and I looked up and my chute was full of holes. To get me down, I had a spot picked out, but the wind caught my chute and drifted me over into the trees. I broke a bunch of branches coming down and the canopy caught up on the top of the tree. I was still about seven feet off the ground. Couldn't get my knee up to get my knife to cut myself free. I was watching branches drop. I thought, well, this is it now.

But two Brits came along, one lifted the other one up. He grabbed my ankles and the weight of the three of us pulled my canopy clear and we ended up in a heap on the ground. So I got out of the harness quickly and then ran to catch up to where we were supposed to be and put in an assault on a farmhouse. We would put an attack in on a village and they'd open up and then we'd attack them and then find out they'd gone to the next village. We covered about three hundred miles. We would ride tanks one day, trucks one day and we'd keep up with the trucks the third day. We came to a place called Wismar on the Baltic. The front of the column came under fire. We all jumped over the side of the trucks and ran to the houses on each side.

Now, there were all hedges with gates in front of the houses, so I burst through this gate, saw movement, fired and then got the shock of my life. A whole line of German youth got up in uniforms—they had bazookas, machine guns, and everything. Their orders were to open up if we were Russians. If we were Americans or Brits, they were to surrender. So I was fortunate again.

Opposite and above: de Vries' boots and fighting knife.

Cyril Roach

BORN » LONDON, ENGLAND

BRANCH » LST-304, ROYAL NAVY

TRADE » ENGINEER OFFICER

HOMETOWN » MISSISSAUGA, ONTARIO

On D-Day—June 6, 1944—"the sea was full of ships as far as the eye could see," including *Landing Ship, Tank (LST) 304*. As the engineer officer in that vessel, Cyril Roach recalls the Allied invasion of Normandy.

I went through training and I became an engineer officer aboard an *LST*, which was a double-decker landing ship that was used at the time of our landings in France. I was a senior, second in command and, of course, we had stokers in the engine room. All of my crew were Canadians from out West, and they did an excellent job. The most important things were the 1,500 horsepower diesels that drove the ship—twin screws. My responsibility was to ensure that we, the equipment, everything, was fully operational.

On D-Day, we arrived in France, having left the Isle of Wight on the night of June 5, about 11 p.m. We arrived off Le Havre, which was in the sector near Ouistreham. This was a point where troops landed with the objective of Caen. The ship dropped the anchor a half a mile out and we then put full speed ahead onto the beaches so that we were able to land the troops and light equipment, which supported also part of the 6th Airborne Division as well as other contingents of the army.

At that time, we were being shelled very heavily from the high ridge over Le Havre, and the sea was full of ships as far as you could see. And there were thousands of aircraft overhead—bombers, fighters, and many of the gliders that were towed in to support the landing of the ground troops.

Shortly after our arrival, we started to unload and there were three Messerschmitts that then strafed the beaches. Regretfully, we lost many men. I also was injured at the time. I survived, I'm happy to say.

The moment we were landing, I thought, whose mother's son dies today? Not just our own boys, but our enemy as well. I learned, unfortunately, that Hitler Youth were in exercise in that general area and those boys were only

> *"The moment we were landing, I thought, whose mother's son dies today? Not just our own boys, but our enemy as well."*

seventeen—just kids. They never saw their homes again. I can't say I was scared. I was just doing my job. And my boys did their job. Like everything else, when you're called into action, you have to concentrate on what you're doing and also ensure that we survived and looked after the boys when we picked them up. But it wasn't a day that one would forget, I assure you.

Top left: Marching band, 1944. Roach performed with a band of the British Home Guard before enlisting in the Royal Navy. He is in the second row, third from the right.

Top right: Roach in Gibraltar, 1946.

Bottom left: British landing ships moving troops up river to Parknam, near Bangkok, Siam, 1945.

Edward Frank "Jiggs" Borland

BORN » READING, PENNSYLVANIA

BRANCH » 14TH CANADIAN HUSSARS
(8TH RECONNAISSANCE REGIMENT), CANADIAN ARMY

TRADE » ARMOURED CAR GUNNER

HOMETOWN » BISHOP'S FALLS, NEWFOUNDLAND AND
LABRADOR

For Jiggs Borland, the "total reality" of war set in when he witnessed a corpse floating in the English Channel en route to Normandy in July 1944. Borland saw extensive action in Europe as an armoured car gunner with the 14th Canadian Hussars, the reconnaissance unit of the 2nd Canadian Infantry Division. He and his two crewmates spearheaded the liberation of Dieppe on September 1, 1944.

In Normandy, in early July 1944, there was one fellow walking across from my trench to another trench in the centre of the field. He was just ready to jump into the trench when a shell struck him right in the chest. It blew him all to smithereens and he fell right into the trench on another fellow and that fellow went berserk. He was sitting there eating his lunch, out of his mess tins and, oh boy, what a mess.

Everybody was standing around stunned—this was our first casualty—and the officer, Major Port, just came charging out and yelled, "Come on, you silly SOBs, get this mess cleaned up quickly and get back to your trenches." Well, to him it was just a mess. It was the right thing to do, of course, shock us back into reality, but if somebody had had a gun they'd have shot him right then and there.

That's the way we had to be treated. I mean, you had to be treated that way or you would go right stark raving mad worrying about it. We got talking to some of the pilots of the Thunderbolt planes, the Hurricanes that used to be over us. They were telling us that the smell from the battlefields could be smelled up six and seven and eight hundred feet in the air.

I remember a strange little incident that happened [in Rouen], down on the one side where the houses all run toward the river. We drove down one of those side streets and we're parked there. The woman in the house came out to the officer. "Sir," she says, "can I feed two of your men?" And he said, "You don't want to have to feed our men, we have lots of food and everything else." "No, no," she says, "I have two children and one is seven and the

*"Just as we tipped down into Dieppe, well, my God,
there's wall-to-wall people dancing and screaming
and banners, and oh my."*

Top: Borland on top of his armoured car, April 1945.
Bottom: On leave in Paris, 1945. Borland is kneeling, fourth from the right.

other is nine, a boy and a girl. I'd take it as a real honour if
you could allow me to feed two of your soldiers."

So he picked us two young fellows, a fellow named
Cripps and myself. And Trooper Cripps and I were told to
mind our manners. And we were very mannerly, very well-
behaved. We went into this woman's house and we had
supper with them. I remember the loaf of bread she had
there, a big round loaf. And every time she'd cut a slice of
bread off, she was crossing—Father, Son, and Holy Ghost.
They were tremendously Catholic in Rouen.

We had a nice little cream pudding and a couple of little
slices of meat and some vegetables and tomatoes—it was
a lovely little lunch. And she was quite pleased. She took
our names and addresses and everything else. I never did
get back to this woman.

Another time, about three miles out of Dieppe: We're
getting there and we'd already been talking to Dieppe by
phone. And they know we're coming. Well, you can imagine what that meant. Just as we tipped down into Dieppe,

well, my God, there's wall-to-wall people dancing and screaming and banners, and oh my. And there's Resistance fellows hanging all over the armoured cars. They'd been hanging on for the last ten miles. Each car had about ten of them, and their little armbands and their little Sten guns and little black berets. Looked kind of cute.

Just as we get over there, I see the smaller armoured car ahead of me is engulfed with people, and then I can see the officer talking to the Resistance fellows. Then the officer picks up his radio. "Jiggs," he said, "get around me now and get down in town. These guys will show you where it is. There's a machine-gun nest, a German machine-gun nest. Go get it, will you."

Now, a nine-ton armoured car is all cast iron so it's pretty safe. I went past them and that's how come I happened to be the first one into Dieppe. And I got down on it [the nest] with the gun and I was going to take out that window when all of a sudden, there were pillow slips and bedsheets waving, "Don't shoot, don't shoot!" And

a policeman came over with his buddy and told me that the Resistance fellows had captured the three Germans on the machine gun and had them outside the wall, and were going to shoot them. I said, "Why were they going to shoot them?" He said, "Well, because they're Germans!" "Is that the only reason you shoot them, is because they're German?" He said, "Oh, absolutely."

We took them. We took them and put them in jail to save their lives. At that moment, a civilian photographer snapped the picture of me. I'm on the radio, I'm sending a message back down the line: "Francis is alive and well." Francis was the code name for Dieppe. "Francis is alive and well, we will expect his friends for dinner." That told the people down the line that Dieppe is liberated, you can send the infantry in now.

Left: The liberation of Dieppe, September 1, 1944. Borland is on the radio.
Above: The Knight of the Legion of Honour (Republic of France), awarded to Borland for his role in the liberation of Dieppe, July 1, 2006.

J.A. René Brunette

BORN » EASTVIEW, ONTARIO

BRANCH » HMCS HEPATICA AND HMCS LA HULLOISE,
ROYAL CANADIAN NAVY

TRADE » SAILOR

HOMETOWN » GATINEAU, QUEBEC

A francophone in a predominantly English-speaking branch of the military, J.A. René Brunette's experience reflects the camaraderie of naval service, a connection fostered by the close quarters on Royal Canadian Navy corvettes and frigates. The cohesion between him and his comrades helped result in the sinking of the German submarine *U-1302* in March 1945.

I was French-speaking and we knew a little bit of English but not a lot! At our house, we read newspapers like *Le Devoir* and *Le Journal*, and my father always worked in French and English, so we had a general idea. But in my line of work, I would say that it was often the English-speaking people who gave me a chance. When I boarded the ship, there were two gentlemen from Ottawa: one named Bonham and one named Burke. The coxswain, who was the assistant officer and in charge of all of the people, he approached me and he said, "If you have any trouble with those English, you tell me, Brunette!" But he

was English-speaking himself—his last name was Cunningham and he was from Dorval (Quebec).

They sent us to Sydney, Nova Scotia, to board our ship. When we got there, we had to sleep in a big garage that had beds set up on benches. The next morning when we got up and looked outside, there was a big ship called a corvette. The corvette was called HMCS *Hepatica*. It wasn't very wide—thirty feet wide and two hundred feet long—and there were over seventy people aboard, so it was a bit cramped! There was a device called sonar, which was placed on the bottom of the ship. It was something like a barrel under the ship that sent frequencies underwater and received them back four times faster than they were sent out, so that we could detect a whale or a submarine or an old shipwreck or anything like that. It was very handy.

When the German submarines detected our supply ships, one by one, they had a chance to shoot. So Mr. Churchill (British Prime Minister) decided that no ship should ever go out alone from any given place; they had to

HMCS *La Hulloise.*

go out together in convoys. Sometimes there were up to twenty submarines that banded together in a group to try and stop our convoys. We managed to slip out to protect our ships. Often people say that it was the air force that won the battle, but in our opinion, it was us—the [merchant] marine and the navy—who helped to save England. If we hadn't been able to bring over the food supplies, the munitions, the shells, and other things like that, then the air force wouldn't have been able to move. Oil, gas, things like that; we provided the support. In my opinion, we were the backbone of the entire organization.

Some of the frigates were built in Canada and they were given the names of cities as often as possible. They were a bit bigger and faster than the other ships. The HMCS *La Hulloise* was a frigate that had 150 sailors aboard. It was more modern and was equipped with everything imaginable; sonar and we even had something new, a grenade called the "hedgehog" [an anti-submarine weapon]. It was installed on the ship's front deck, in front of both can-

nons. It was about twenty inches long and three inches in diameter, and it could launch grenades ahead at submarines when they were close.

We were escorting ships to cities such as Liverpool and Southampton and places like that. We were three ships together, two others and us, and we received an order to go patrol the Irish Sea around the northwest coast of Ireland. So we departed northwards and at around eleven o'clock at night, the radar picked up something. It indicated that there was a submarine ahead of us. We didn't think that it could be possible. We were so close to the coast that we could see the red lights on the buoys, like on the Ottawa River. The captain said, "How could it be?" And then the radar repeated its signal. So then we did something that we were never supposed to do during a time of war, but the captain took a chance—we approached and the captain turned on a huge spotlight so that we could clearly see the submarine. When it saw us, and the light from the spotlight, it started to descend—to "crash," you could say—to

"[W]e did something that we were never supposed to do during a time of war, but the captain took a chance—we approached and the captain turned on a huge spotlight so that we could clearly see the submarine."

the bottom of the bay. So we relayed the coordinates to the two other boats that were with us and we started dropping depth charges on them.

After a few minutes, we saw some flotsam come up through the water. The attack lasted about forty minutes, all in all, and then we started patrolling the waters again until the following morning. The next day, we went back to see if there were any survivors and there were none. There were forty dead sailors. We even picked up a notebook that included a letter that a young sailor was undoubtedly writing to his mother. He thought that he would be home for Easter. It was March 8 [1945]. I will never forget that date, since my mother's birthday is the following day. A lot of us cried and prayed for them—we were all under a lot of pressure. We figured out that there were forty-four men aboard.

Crew of HMCS *La Hulloise*. Brunette is in the centre row, fifth from the right.

LA HULLOISE

Francis

A Métis fror
Beach. He w
nearly a year

I went out v
hardly spe
The school w
wouldn't take
to go in the
called you a
they were.

I had no
working in tl
I knew I cou
for the army
tigues, wash
complaining
I enlisted in

We stayec

Jim Brown

BORN » FREDERICTON, NEW BRUNSWICK

BRANCH » HMCS MONNOW, ROYAL CANADIAN NAVY

TRADE » ANTI-AIRCRAFT GUNNER

HOMETOWN » LINCOLN, NEW BRUNSWICK

An eighteen-year-old New Brunswicker from the tiny land-locked community of Lincoln, Jim Brown enlisted in the navy in 1943. He served aboard the frigate HMCS *Monnow* as an Oerlikon gunner, once shooting down a German Junkers 88 on the dangerous run between Britain and the Soviet Arctic port of Murmansk. The Soviet government later decorated Brown for his service.

When we finished our training in Cornwallis they took us aboard the HMCS *Beaver*, a little training ship. They took us across the Bay of Fundy to Saint John and it was rough, I'm telling' you, it was rough. A lot of people were sick. We stayed overnight in Saint John and then the next day we boarded again and went back to Cornwallis. That was our sea time, other than a whaler here and there.

I was on a gunner's party so I had to clean guns. My ordnance artificer—who was the head of the gunnery thing onboard our ship—he would come to me and say,

"Jim, where did you get that piece?" He said," I've never seen it before." These were twenty-millimetres we'd take apart, you see, 'cause they were up in the air where the seawater might get splashed on them and you had to take them apart and grease them and clean them.

Our food, far as I'm concerned, was perfect. I've heard army guys talk about, no, they didn't have this, they didn't have that, but we had everything. None of us went hungry, and when we'd come into port there'd be these great big wicker baskets full of fresh bread, cream cans full of fresh milk. That was sure a treat when you'd come into port.

If it was really rough at sea, they'd put a great big square tin on top of the stove, about twelve inches high, I suppose, and about two-and-a-half, three inches square. And they'd fill that full of canned tomatoes and bacon—we'd call it "red lead and bacon." That's what they'd have when the sea was rough, 'cause it could just stay in this big thing and cook on top of the stove.

We were the first convoy to make it to Murmansk with-

HMCS *Monnow*'s boarding party, guarding prisoners on a German U-boat.
Top right: U-boats that surrendered to the Allies off Norway on May 17, 1945.
Centre: Dog tag.
Bottom right: German U-boat, May 1945.

"I waited and waited and waited until he got in within range and I opened fire with my twenty-millimetre and he just disappeared, went down into the sea."

out losing a ship. It was quite a run. We had a big convoy. I don't recall the exact number now, but it seems to me there was forty-five naval ships, and something like eighty-five merchant ships. We had fifty tons of medical supplies in our gangways down below and that went to Russia. All these medical supplies, and I suppose that's the reason I got a medal from Russia.

We started to stay away from the Norwegian coast because that's where the Germans were. Got one of them—I shot one down coming back. On the Murmansk run you don't get much daylight, especially in the wintertime. When we were coming back they were coming at us a little bit, they hit empty ships coming back from Russia. We just happened to be in a spot where I was on watch at the time. We closed up because they were hitting the ships behind us. And it just happened I looked in the sky and I saw a plane coming—a silhouette in the sky. I waited and waited and waited until he got in within range and I opened fire with my twenty-millimetre and he just dis-

appeared, went down into the sea. I looked on the other side and there was another one coming. I hollered to the fellow on the other side of the ship. I said, "wait, wait, let him get in range because your twenty-millimetre is not good enough for that distance, you know." But he started firing and the plane went off. He didn't get him.

You go through all this stuff and you're drilled into it day after day after day, and then all of a sudden you're out of it. And there's nobody hollering at you, and you don't have to run, and you don't have to salute. I remember when we first started out we were saluting streetcar conductors in Saint John. It takes you a bit of getting used to, it's just like starting to live over again.

HMCS *Monnow*, 1945, and an HMCS *Monnow* crest.

John Marchand

BORN » VERNON, BRITISH COLUMBIA

BRANCH » THE LANARK AND RENFREW SCOTTISH
REGIMENT, CANADIAN ARMY

TRADE » BREN GUNNER

HOMETOWN » VERNON, BRITISH COLUMBIA

John Marchand enlisted in the army in January 1943, initially joining the Royal Canadian Artillery. After arriving in Italy, the desperate need for infantry reinforcements in theatre resulted in the young Aboriginal's transfer to the newly established Lanark and Renfrew Scottish Regiment as a Bren gunner.

Our first job was crossing this river [in Italy], attacking. And lieutenants and sergeant-majors are telling us, "Oh, it's just an ordinary river. It might be ten feet deep in some places, but if you want to take a big running jump, you'll hit land, in the water." I was a Bren gunner, a machine gunner, and they said, "keep your arms up out of the water if you can." We had these pouches, with Bren clips in them, and we had our packs on our back with food and spare socks and things like that. Then you have your water bottle on the side and your first-aid thing on your front. I take a running jump, and hit nothing. By the time I got to the bank, they were already shooting in our direction. This was two o'clock in the morning.

I emptied all the water and everything and put [the gun] back together again. The guy next to me said that there were flashes coming out of a building, and to get them first. Every machine gun has a tracer bullet—a light—and you'd have to shoot at those lights. And that's what I was doing. I'd shoot at them, empty a whole round and get a new one, put it in and then they'd spray us. The shrubs along the banks, you could hear them just breaking and being hit by bullets. There'd be another blast and somebody would say, "Oh yeah, on the left," and I'd fire at that. And then that would go out. Then over here, another one, in the same place again. And it was like that for, oh, I don't know, half an hour. And that was our first fight as infantry.

Inland from Ravenna was an intersection. The tanks had already gotten to that part—armoured services, all the trucks, the supplies. We went through, at two o'clock in the morning, to go further ahead past them. We got halfway across the field and were shelled. There was a ditch

"The shrubs along the banks, you could hear them just breaking and being hit by bullets."

Left: Marchand at the Vernon Army Camp, British Columbia, 1942.
Right: Marchand and his mother Helene, 1942.

"It hit so close that it popped you right out of your little [fox]hole—popped you right out and moved you over about five or six feet."

across the field where they were firing at us from, so we just dug in right there. When there got to be enough daylight so our artillery could see where they were, we started shelling that part. But we didn't move until the following evening, when it got dark again.

There was a little building that they used, maybe for storing their equipment or something, and we crawled into it, to have a bite and to bandage up some guys that had arm cuts or leg cuts or whatever. Anyway, I was in there, and this soldier, his name was Leroy, he walked out for some reason. As soon as they saw somebody move, they started shooting at him. Of course, they hit him. We brought him back in. We gave him morphine, but he was bleeding from his chest and his back. We put all of our bandages on him.

By that time, we got word to the medics. So two of them came and put him on a stretcher and took him away. From there we moved up to the next ditch. The German tanks started firing at us again. Then they started peppering us with mortars. And that's the nearest I got to being hurt, I guess. It hit so close that it popped you right out of your little [fox]hole—popped you right out and moved you over about five or six feet. And you couldn't hear, you couldn't see, you couldn't breathe. You had to crawl back into the hole again.

We called for artillery guns and this time, air support. Once they started dive-bombing them, the guys went through us and ahead. On our way back to the intersection, which they were shelling, guys were going from one side of the road to the other side. The shrapnel would take someone's leg off and he'd hop across and dive off the road. We saw stuff like that: these crazy guys going from one side of the road to the other, being peppered with artillery. That was our last real fight.

Opposite left: Marchand, nineteen years old, home from a logging camp, Vernon, British Columbia, summer 1940.
Opposite right: Marchand and his sister Florence, embarkation leave, 1942.

Maurice White

BORN » EDMONTON, ALBERTA

BRANCH » CANADIAN PROVOST CORPS; THE LOYAL
EDMONTON REGIMENT, CANADIAN ARMY;
1ST SPECIAL SERVICE FORCE, UNITED STATES ARMY

TRADE » INFANTRYMAN

HOMETOWN » EDMONTON, ALBERTA

Initially a military policeman, Maurice White served in Italy and the south of France with the Loyal Edmonton Regiment and then the "Devil's Brigade," the famous Canada-U.S. First Special Service Force.

I landed in Sicily on July 10, 1943. I think I was the fifth man ashore in my company. There was very little action. The Italians were supposed to be looking after that part of the coast, but they were not very anxious to fight. The first dead soldier I saw was just near the beach—an Italian soldier. I remember that very plainly. I can see his body laying on the ground, and there was kind of a liquor smell, I still don't know what it was. But every time I smell that smell, I see that body. It's funny how smell will preserve your memory.

I fought all the way through Sicily. I only missed one battle and that was the last one we fought: Hill 736. From there, we went to mainland Italy and landed in Reggio Calabria. I fought up through the boot. I spent Christmas Day in Ortona. We went in under a creeping barrage on December 20. We entered the southern part of the village and spent the night in a soap factory, I think it was. The next morning, things really started to happen. It took us eight days to finally take the town. We had to go from one room to the other. We'd blow a hole in the side of the house and go in through it because the streets were filled with rubble and machine guns. You were signing your death warrant to go out on the street.

On Christmas Day, things were kind of slowing down a little bit. I had found a position up in the east end of a house, and had knocked out two bricks so I could observe the square behind the house. I was eating my Christmas dinner there. They brought up hot food for us—I don't know how they got it up there, but they did—I think it was hot pork and gravy, mashed potatoes, and a bottle of beer. I had taken this up to my lookout post and, as a matter of fact, I shot a German on Christmas day. At the time, it didn't bother me, but ever since, I've thought, why did I

do that? It was Christmas day. I shouldn't have, but maybe then it would have been him shooting at me. You don't have a choice, you either shoot somebody or they shoot you.

"I can see his body laying on the ground, and there was kind of a liquor smell, I still don't know what it was. But every time I smell that smell, I see that body."

When I shot him, he fell, and two German soldiers came out and grabbed him. I didn't shoot back. I thank God that I didn't. That would have been even worse to handle. So that was Christmas day—one of the very unpleasant things you regret later on.

Above: White in England at the end of the war.
Top right: White with his brother Alec (left) in 1942.
Bottom right: White while serving in the Canadian Provost Corps.

Eric "Lofty" Saunders

BORN » BATTLE, ENGLAND

BRANCH » NO. 41 ROYAL MARINE COMMANDO,
BRITISH ROYAL MARINES

TRADE » COMMANDO

HOMETOWN » WASAGA BEACH, ONTARIO

Eric Saunders was born in Battle, East Sussex, the site of the Battle of Hastings, William of Normandy's victory over the English King Harold II in 1066. Saunders experienced the reverse engagement, taking part in the D-Day landings, where he was gravely wounded on Sword Beach.

It was from a little place called Duntroon, Scotland, that we boarded a ship one day and headed for the Middle East. We didn't know what to expect, but it turned out to be the Sicily landings. That was our first experience with action.

After Sicily was taken, we were drawn back out and put in a holding area for a while. We were told that our services would no longer be required there—we'd be going back to England. But it didn't happen that way. They decided to make a raid at a place called Salerno, just partway up Italy. We were supposed to have gone in to the Salerno Valley and cut off the Germans from behind, cut off their supplies. That turned out to be a pretty bad deal. We didn't know at the time, but sitting up in the hills around the Salerno Valley was a huge German concentration—a panzer [German armoured] division.

We landed at night at a place called Vietri [sul-Mare]. It was built, more or less, on the side of a hill. We went in almost unopposed, climbed up through Vietri and out into the valley on the other side. And there we took our positions in amongst the grapevines, dug in, and waited for daylight. When daylight arrived, we started to move around. That's when we found out that the Germans were looking right down on us. They just let us have it. We were head to head, and we lost a lot of men. And we had to dig in deeper and find what cover we could. We were there for several days.

Other troops had landed a little farther south, on the other side of the valley, and we had to wait for them to come up. It took them several days to make it. In the meantime, we had been beaten up pretty badly. They withdrew us all on one day. There was a huge viaduct that ran across this valley. There was a bit of cover there, so they drove us all

back under these arches and we reformed the unit. Out of what was six troops, we now had just three.

The idea was that we were going to assault this German position. So we formed up and took up a position in the foothills. There was a huge barrage that came down from the naval guns onto the German position—or it should have been on the German position. Something went wrong and one salvo landed right in the middle of us. That killed a lot of our guys, but we still rallied. We eventually went up into the hills and we did manage to rout the Germans out of there. That was quite a happy ending to that deal, except for all the men that were lost.

Eventually we set sail and got out into the Atlantic. We ran into a German wolf pack [a German U-boat tactic designed to attack convoys]. They chased us all over the place. We lost two or three boats, and the convoy was told to break up and make their own way. Our ship, being one of the faster ones, took off. All you could hear when you were down below was tick, tick, and a big explosion.

Left: January 1942.
Right: Saunders' comrades from No. 41 Royal Marine Commando, X Troop, Sicily, 1943.

"When I came to, all I could see was a ring of red bloody faces and guys were screaming for their mother."

These were depth charges going off. We eventually outran the pack and got away clean. We arrived in Glasgow eight days later and went up the Clyde [River] and anchored for the night. They had an air raid there. One of the boats right next to us sank. A lot of guys that had been rescued on the convoy were lost.

When we got to Portsmouth, we knew that something big was going to happen because there were hundreds of troops around. We were put in a big park under [orders of] strict silence. We went aboard ship in Portsmouth, a landing craft, and away we went to France. We landed on D-Day. I made it to the top of the beach, I don't know how. The machine-gun fire was unbelievable, and the shells and mortars. I got to the top of the beach and got down behind a sand dune. I looked around. Most of my guys were scattered around there behind me, so I moved along the beach a little bit to join up with another two or three guys.

We were just getting ready to fire at these machine guns. They were in a large building overlooking the beach, and every window had a machine gun in it, I think. But just as we were doing that, there was a big boom and that was it for me; that was the end of it. I don't remember very much for a few seconds. When I came to, all I could see was a ring of red bloody faces and guys were screaming for their mother. A guy grabbed me and pulled me away. Eventually, we got back down to the waterline and they took us up toward one of the landing craft.

I went back to England and spent a few months in the hospital. Eventually, I went to a camp that they had formed up in North Wales—a convalescent camp. I started doing a bit more training, exercising things, but I never really got fit enough to go back. They called me in one day, along with three or four other NCOs [non-commissioned officers], and said, "We would like you to go down to our training area and see if you could do some recruiting for the commandos." That's where I went and that's where I spent the rest of the war.

COMMANDO SERVICE CERTIFICATE

Italy · Crete · Burma · Greece
Norway · France · Sicily · Albania
Holland · Belgium · Germany · Madagascar
North Africa · Yugoslavia · Western Desert · Channel Islands

This Certificate is an Appreciation,
of Loyal Service given to Commandos by

Po/x 105859 Mne Saunders E. (Royal Marines)

12th March 194 6

Chief of Combined Operations

Served in Commandos from October 1942 to February 1946

12th March 194 6

Lt Col R.M.

Top: Members of No. 41 Royal Marine Commando, in
1943, just before leaving Scotland for Sicily.

Bottom: Salerno War Cemetery, Italy, 1989.

Above: Commando service certificate, presented
March 12, 1946.

Malcolm Andrade

BORN » GEORGETOWN, BRITISH GUIANA

BRANCH » NO. 91 AND NO. 127 SQUADRONS, ROYAL AIR FORCE

TRADE » PILOT

HOMETOWN » BURLINGTON, ONTARIO

Malcolm Andrade enlisted in the Royal Air Force in September 1943. A Spitfire pilot with the Second Tactical Air Force, he closely supported the Allied armies in Normandy and Northwest Europe, particularly during the fighting to close the Falaise Gap in August 1944. Andrade also fondly recalls "the guys I flew with" and the welcome he and his comrades received from the Belgian and Dutch people.

The main idea of the tactical air force was to support the armies in the field. That was their job. Their job wasn't to go fighter to fighter. Their job was to support the armies. So they had bombers, they had fighters of different types. And their job was to harass the Germans behind the lines. Particularly at the dictation of the army groups. So we were constantly on demand by the army.

One operation is very, very strong in my memory—and that was when we attacked a column of the SS. They were the elite and ruthless bunch. And we were given the order to attack them, which we did—a surprise attack. We fired on them from all angles, continuously. One of the members there was on a motorcycle—probably a dispatch rider—and he took off from the column, because we were strafing it. You normally bomb one end and bomb the other end and have them blocked in so that you could get at them without them being able to move very much. A lot of the troops were getting out of the transports and running into the fields. But this guy took off and I went with another one of my wingmen and we went after this guy. So here he is, let's say he's doing, I don't know, maybe seventy miles an hour, and we're doing about 290. So, what did he think he was doing? Looking back on it, maybe he had urgent dispatches. I have no idea, maybe he just plain panicked. But I remember coming up on this fellow and we just blew him apart.

When the Allies overran that particular position, they asked us if we wanted to go down and see the damage we'd done. They took us out there to have a look... [it was] pretty bad, pretty bad when you see it close up. The smell

"[T]hey saw the roundels on our aircraft and they said we were freedom, that's what we were."

NATIONAL REGISTRATION IDENTITY CARD

NUMBER: WNCR 1 : 86
SURNAME: ANDRADE
CHRISTIAN NAMES (First only in full): Malcolm S.
CLASS CODE: B 273
FULL POSTAL ADDRESS: Prior Park College, Bath
HOLDER'S SIGNATURE: Malcolm Stephen Andrade
CHANGES OF ADDRESS. No entry except by National Registration Officer, to whom removal must be notified.

CITY OF BATH.

CIVIL DEFENCE.

This is to Certify that

M Andrade
Prior Park College

is a member of a Fire-fighting party organised by the Bath City Council, and possesses the powers of entry and of taking steps for extinguishing fire or for protecting property or rescuing persons or property from fire, which are conferred by the Fire Precautions (Access to Premises) (No. 2) Order, 1941.

Authorising Officer.
Town Clerk.
Date 3/2/43

No. 3130
Folio No. 4149
Trained—Stage I. 21-1-43
Stage II. 28-1-43
Block No.

CITY OF BATH
FIRE GUARD SERVICE.

Above: Royal Air Force Officer's Cap Badge.

was terrible. The smell of death, rotting, burnt. Not pleasant. Something you never forget, you absolutely never forget the smell.

We used to fly in Holland, and also partly in Belgium and France. Our base was basically a field in the middle of farm country, and many a time you'd come back and see all these kids and sometimes adults cycling along on their bicycles. When they heard the engines coming, they nearly fell off their bikes waving to us. It was very moving. I always remember one kid; he collided with the bike in front of him and fell off. I could just get the glimpse of him as I swept past, and here he was scrambling to his feet to continue waving. These little things get to you. Talking to them way after the war, you find out that they saw the roundels on our aircraft and they said we were freedom, that's what we were.

A lot of the guys we lost, some were wounded, some missing. And some of the carnage you saw and carried out yourself. It comes back to you and it's a hell of a thing

to say, but when you're in combat, you're being fired at, you get all fired up yourself and you give it back to them as best you can, as much as you get, you give it back to them. You know, you look back on it, and, you're killing people, so it's kind of tough, and you're losing people. After a while you don't really want to get too close to anybody. Because they're here today, gone tomorrow, as you could be. You're chummy and you're friendly and you go out to the pubs and have a bash and it's good fun, but very few people really got to know me, very few people.

I've always remembered those years extremely fondly, and the people I flew with. I still keep in touch with one or two. It's very vivid, that part of my life. Very exciting, I have to tell you, at the time it was very exciting and scary...scary.

Left: France, late 1944, with Spitfires in the background.
Above: France and Germany Star; War Medal (1939–45).

CONNECTIONS

The nation was represented in its forces overseas with Canadians from every class and region, brought together in the hothouse environment of a closed society. Canadians had a strong attachment to their service arm, but also their regiment, ship, aircraft or support unit. Traditions, training, and leadership helped to hold the formation together, even in the cauldron of battle, but the ultimate glue was one's comrades—second families formed of men and women who shared the same trials and deprivations, who witnessed heroism and horror, who experienced similar fear and trauma.

These families, built up over months, could be torn apart in minutes. Ships that were sunk could lose most of their crew; artillery batteries smothered by counter-battery shellfire might be destroyed in the blink of an eye; tanks were hit—"brewed up"—and their crews roasted alive, with usually only a lucky few managing to escape their crude crematorium. The stress at the front was unimaginable, but most Canadians held on past the breaking point because of the comrade next to them: to flee or stop functioning would be akin to abandoning one's family. These intense bonds, these connections, kept the forces fighting.

Canadians overseas also remained deeply connected to their families, friends, and communities. Tens of millions of letters passed back and forth over the oceans—missives of love and longing, of unspoken fear and forced banalities. Carefully inscribed words or hastily scribbled notes were often the only messages received over a period of years. How are you getting on? Are my parents helping you? How could one describe the deep emptiness of missing children, of parents aching for the return of an absent son or daughter, of a wife's anxiety and loneliness as she struggled to care for her family? It was hard to share experiences in five hundred words; it was impossible to communicate a smile, a wink, a caress on the arm. Some men were gone for up to six years, and many relationships could not stand the strain. Yet thousands did.

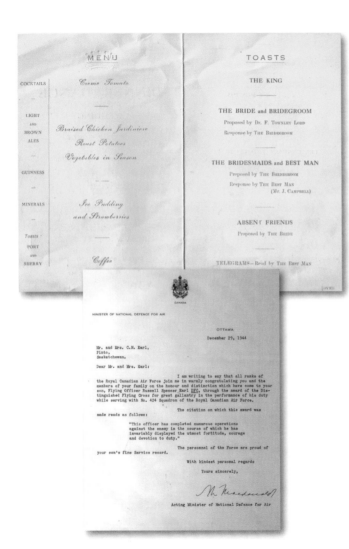

Half a million Canadians were stationed in the United Kingdom during the war. These young men lived for the moment; it was all they might have. Towards the end of the war, in the Netherlands, the Canadian liberators were wealthy, healthy, and randy. The starving female population often responded generously, seeking to fill needs and wants. In 1946, there were more than seven thousand illegitimate births recorded in the Netherlands, double the previous year's number.

There were also long-term relationships. Canadian liberators in France and the Netherlands remembered saving and feeding children, and some stayed in touch for decades. Some fifty thousand war brides and thousands of children eventually came to Canada during and after the war, setting up a new life in a new country. While the challenges for these new families were great, their stories were often among the happiest to come out of the war.

Love and relationships are understandable in wartime England or in liberated Netherlands, but they were generally absent from the battlefield, where the need for survival overruled most normal human impulses. One was expected to hate one's adversaries. That was often the case, but there was also a strange relationship with the enemy, who was part of a shared community of the damned. Ships' crews would pick up survivors from damaged U-boats, even though that same submarine had been trying to send their ship to the bottom of the ocean only minutes earlier. Front-line soldiers faced off against each other and were the ones most likely to kill at close and personal ranges, but even in this brutal environment, mercy, and sometimes tenderness, were often extended to the enemy. Behind the lines, prisoners of war were usually treated generously, while wounded enemy soldiers were cared for by nurses and doctors.

Following the war, Canadian survivors returned to the changed nation that they helped to forge. Many veterans kept in touch with their wartime comrades through letters or occasional reunions; the legion halls acted as places of refuge and provided an opportunity to hoist a pint, tell a tall tale, hum an old song, or remember a fallen comrade. The war had seen too many friends put into shallow graves, but most survivors found lifelong comrades, with whom they shared a deep, unbreakable bond.

Top: Molly P. Corby and William B. Campbell's Wedding Program, June 5, 1948.
Bottom: Letter from the Minister of National Defence for Air to Russell Earl's parents, congratulating their son on the award of his Distinguished Flying Cross, December 29, 1944.

Ross Hamilton

BORN » SUNDRIDGE, ONTARIO

BRANCH » NO. 407 (DEMON) SQUADRON,
ROYAL CANADIAN AIR FORCE

TRADE » WIRELESS AIR GUNNER

HOMETOWN » KELOWNA, BRITISH COLUMBIA

A wireless air gunner with No. 407 (Demon) Squadron, one of the first Royal Canadian Air Force squadrons to see service in Europe, Ross Hamilton's story emphasizes both the dangers of war and some of the humorous ways of coping with those dangers. Fear was a constant companion, overcome both by disciplinary measures such as "a very, very black mark... called lack of moral fibre," and by loyalty between comrades.

I enlisted in the air force as soon as I was eighteen. Eventually, we were posted to the 407 Squadron in North Devon, [England] which was one of the first Canadian squadrons to be formed overseas during the war. Their initial task was to deal with the shipping strikes off the Dutch coast in the North Sea.

Wing Commander Ken Wilson was an RMC [Royal Military College] graduate, pre-war pilot, and commanding officer of our squadron. He called us in and said he had a request from Air Ministry in London to dispatch a crew to a fighter station in Sussex, RAF Station Ford, to carry out some secret duties. He picked us because we had a good reputation on the squadron and a top-notch pilot. He didn't ask us if we wanted to go, we were just told we were going there. So we took off for Ford a couple of days later having no idea what we were going to. When we landed, we were met by the station adjutant, who took us to his office and gave each of us a Bible and we swore on it that we would tell nothing of what we were doing there.

The German aircraft were carrying buzz bombs [V1 rockets] over to the coast and launching them on England. The bases they were launched from had been virtually wiped out by Bomber Command, so the Germans had to find some way of getting the bombs to England. They invented this idea of putting a big V1 rocket onto a Heinkel [He] 111, flying it across the [English] Channel at zero height almost, so it wouldn't be detected by radar from the shore. They would climb up to 1,500 feet as they neared the English coast and launch it at London. Then they would drop

down to zero feet again and head for home, if they weren't caught. Our duty was with the long-range radar—it was good for about twenty miles. We were to pick these Heinkel 111s up as they come up to altitude. We would have a night fighting [de Havilland] Mosquito or a [Bristol] Beaufighter tailing along behind us and we'd give him a course to steer. He would call back eventually and say, "Tally-ho, I have him." And he would then attack the Heinkel 111 and shoot it down before it launched its missiles.

We did a lot of night patrols. It was always at night because the enemy would only send the Heinkel 111s out in the worst possible weather. I think of it a lot, and I can recall cases where there were accidents, for example on a station, and aircraft crashing and people killed. Those are some of the most vivid memories I have—the terror of that was worse than what we were doing.

Top: Mosquito at RAF Station Ford, Sussex, England.
Bottom: Crew of No. 407 Squadron, RAF Station Chivenor, 1944. Hamilton is fourth from the left.

It was a brotherhood and a fraternity like no other. And it was just, I'm doing it, so the other guys are doing it too. So what, you know? I better not show any fear about it. And if you did have any fear, why, it was detected very quickly by the station medical officer and you were grounded. And then you got a very, very black mark against you called "lack of moral fibre." And that was more disgraceful than anything. So you were very careful about that. If you were scared, you didn't show it.

We almost got court-martialled, the second pilot and myself, for having a party one night in the mess at Coggeshall [England]. We were the only Canadians at Coggeshall at the time. Robbie and I got on our bikes and we rode out into the countryside to a tree that he had spotted, full of chickens. And to make a long story short, in the court they said we murdered half a dozen of these chickens, one for each member of the crew and brought them back to the barracks. They did a real thorough detective job when they found bits and pieces of blue battle-dress uniform on some

"It was a brotherhood and a fraternity like no other."

of the brambles where we'd disembowelled these chickens. And they knew it was Canadian material and they knew right where to come. We ended up in court and it was like a murder trial, because food was so scarce and so rationed and here we were hijacking chickens off a farm.

The lady judge gave us a real dressing down, told us we were a disgrace to our uniforms and all that stuff and she fined each of us ten pounds. I think Robbie had the cheque written out before she got the last words out of her mouth. Then she asked the group captain if he had anything to say. He gave quite a narrative of the fact that we were there helping England in the war and that we had done something wrong and we should be forgiven for it. And he went on and on and on praising us. And we were almost in tears, what wonderful guys we were! And then he ended up by saying, if these gentlemen are convicted

Crews from No. 407 Squadron at RAF Station Chivenor, 1944. Hamilton is third on left in the front row.

here in the court, then they'll have to go before a district court martial and we'll probably be sent back to Canada disgraced. Then, he said, "You and I and all of England will lose their valuable services for the rest of the war." Well, that got the jury and the judge really good I guess, so we ended up with just a fine.

The ending of it all was that evening. We went to the mess for dinner and we took a carton of cigarettes each because relatives at home in Canada could send you a carton every month for a dollar. Robbie and I each took a carton over to the group captain. They loved their Canadian cigarettes because theirs were rationed. He was playing snooker in the mess, and we went over to him and told him that we wanted to give him a carton of cigarettes and thank him for his efforts on our behalf. So he accepted them, he said, "I guess I can accept these. It doesn't look as though it's a bribe anymore because this case is done with." He thanked us and as we were leaving he said, "Oh, gentlemen, don't be late for dinner tonight, they're having chicken."

Hugh Bartley

BORN » HEDDINGLY, MANITOBA
BRANCH » NO. 128 SQUADRON, ROYAL AIR FORCE
TRADE » PILOT
HOMETOWN » MISSISSAUGA, ONTARIO

Hugh Bartley, a Mosquito pilot with No. 128 Squadron of the Royal Air Force, survived the destruction of his aircraft "at night, at twenty-five thousand feet" over Belgium in 1944. His wounds did not stop him from walking down the aisle with Barbara, an English war bride, shortly thereafter.

I married a war bride, my Barbara, who has been married to me for sixty-four years. And this was our second-attempt marriage. The first time I went missing. Barbara had to send back all the wedding gifts and so forth, and then I turned up.

We flew in the Mosquitoes. We flew above the heavy flak, the heavy ground defences. We could go up as high as thirty-thousand [feet]. And also, we were very fast. At that time, the only thing the Germans had that could catch us would be the odd rocket fighter. But they couldn't catch us at night. Our biggest worry was weather.

We crashed in Belgium on the night of September 16, 1944, went down because of weather. We went into a thunderstorm at the top; the weather inside there was violent. Our aircraft was a fine airplane, but it was made of wood and it came apart. This was at night, at twenty-five thousand feet. Mainly you're so busy you don't have time to get scared. You're trying to get out of whatever kind of a problem you got into, and in this case the airplane made it simple for us. My navigator, unfortunately, got killed.

I was in this convalescent hospital and I had got in touch with my Barbara before then, and we rescheduled the marriage for the tenth of December, in Hull in England. The thing I remember in particular about our marriage was coming up the aisle, and I had a cane, and not very much hair, and a few cuts and bruises, and a limp, and my best man had his head swathed in bandages, and a cane and he limped. It was a real wartime wedding.

Sometimes people feel going and bombing all those places in Germany and such, was it really worthwhile, you know? What were we bombing, anyways? Why were we bombing cities? If you're going to fight an all out war,

you can't be too...what's the word...too discrete. Besides which, if you're going to a place like the German Ruhr, which was heavily industrialized, whether you kill the workers, or the plant, where do you cut it off? Where do you say, well we won't go and bomb that plant because there's a bunch of workers in it, you know? We took the view, in many cases, and certainly the British population did, that as you sow, so shall you reap. And we had all been to London and places like that where the East End was all smashed to smithereens. So we didn't have too damn much sympathy.

"The thing I remember in particular about our marriage was coming up the aisle, and I had a cane, and not very much hair, and a few cuts and bruises, and a limp..."

Gordon Bannerman

BORN » ANEROID, SASKATCHEWAN

BRANCH » 17TH FIELD REGIMENT,
ROYAL CANADIAN ARTILLERY, CANADIAN ARMY

TRADE » GUNNER

HOMETOWN » VICTORIA, BRITISH COLUMBIA

An artillery gunner originally from rural Saskatchewan, Gordon Bannerman rose through the ranks to become a battery sergeant major. While serving with the artillery in Italy and the Netherlands, Bannerman and his comrades developed bonds stronger than those forged in civilian life.

Rome fell June 4, 1944, and Canadians were there until almost the end of June. I was in Rome for July 1, 1944, and I had my mind made that I was going to see the Vatican. As we went up the steps, I said I would like to get a picture taken, and these very good-looking Italian girls came along. I sort of said, in my broken Italian and English, "Come and have your photo taken with me." I never saw them before, they never saw me before, and ten seconds later they were gone.

We went back into action in August for the Gothic Line. There was a tremendous amount of shellfire in most of the areas of a place called Montemaggiore. They just blanketed the valley with mortars coming in by the hundreds, but we survived that until a day or two later when the big railway gun started firing. One of our young fellows was badly wounded, and subsequently passed away. When I bent down over him on the stretcher, I said, "Coyle, just lay still." And he said, "I know you, Gordie." He put his arms around my neck and, well, by the time they put him in the truck to go to an aid post he was gone.

Orme Payne and I went to school together. We played hockey together. We played ball together. We joined the same day. We were both eighteen. And at Otterloo, in Holland, I wondered what happened to Orme. I started across the field and I looked up and there's a figure coming toward me, and here was Orme. We met in the middle of this field and our words were, "By God, I'm glad to see you." He'd heard that I'd been killed the night before. And I saw the house Orme was in go up in fire so I thought that was the end of him too.

The memories of the fellows that I actually served with during those days, it's a bond closer than brothers.

Left: Flanked by two Italian girls on the steps of St. Peter's, July 1, 1944.

Top: Bannerman at home with his father George and sister Marjorie.

Bottom: Bannerman (left) and Sergeant Orme Payne, after seventy-three days in action without being relieved by another unit.

Jean-Marie Milot

BORN » MONTREAL, QUEBEC

BRANCH » LE RÉGIMENT DE LA CHAUDIÈRE, CANADIAN ARMY

TRADE » INFANTRYMAN

HOMETOWN » VAUDREUIL, QUEBEC

As a nineteen-year-old infantryman in 1945, Jean-Marie Milot joined other Canadian and Allied soldiers in the occupation of a defeated Germany. He describes the camaraderie of service life and the dismal conditions in Europe, where "some creatures had to give themselves for cigarettes or to buy things," after six years of war.

As soon as my training was over, so was the war. They sent us by plane to Belgium, then to Holland, and then into Germany. We spent fifteen days on the frontline, and then they transferred us to Holland. After that we formed a third battalion in the Régiment de la Chaudière to occupy Germany.

We went to the town of Zeven, where we spent nine months occupying the area. We had to constantly monitor the area with our rifles loaded, in case anything happened. We weren't allowed to fraternize with anyone. After a period of time, we were able to talk to people, and we didn't have to walk around with our guns anymore; however, we still had to search all the houses to make sure nobody had any guns. There were people and soldiers who didn't report in, so we had to check everyone's papers.

I liked the military life. At fourteen years of age, I entered Les Fusiliers Mont-Royal. I spent two years in college with Les Fusiliers Mont-Royal. I really liked the military aspect. I always appreciated the discipline. Then when the war broke out and I was called to the army, I was pleased to go instead of requesting to be exempted like our foreman suggested. I preferred serving my country. Cigarettes cost eleven cents each, and with a cigarette, you could buy food on the black market. I couldn't believe it! I even bought myself a mandolin with ten cigarettes. It was made in Catania, Italy. So I was walking around with a guitar that I got for cigarettes. And with a guitar, when taking the train, you could sing songs to avoid getting bored.

The only thing I wouldn't want to see is war. There's nothing funny about seeing young people who have to beg for food and they have no clothes. Even some creatures

"We went to the town of Zeven, where we spent nine months occupying the area. We had to constantly monitor the area with our rifles loaded..."

had to give themselves for cigarettes or to buy things. I didn't like seeing that. It's hard for us to imagine, but being there, we saw how willing people were. When we wanted to have our clothes or whatever washed, we went to the fence. People were there who wanted the work, but they didn't have any soap. We had soap though so we put a piece of it through with our clothing, and then the women would fight for the soap and to wash our clothes. If a button or something was missing, they darned it and gave it back to us, and we would give them some soap and a few cigarettes. They weren't afraid of not recognizing us when we came back. It was hard for us you know, since everyone looked the same. How will they know whose clothes belong to who? But they remembered us. We trusted them with our belongings; they were honest people. Even in Germany, during the occupation, it was the same. They were very friendly. Everywhere we went, French Canadians had a good reputation. Everywhere we went, people respected us.

Top: Milot with the mandolin he obtained for ten cigarettes.
Bottom: SS *Ile de France*, a troop ship used to move troops back and forth across the Atlantic.

Albert Hogg

BORN » TORONTO, ONTARIO

BRANCH » THE PRINCESS LOUISE FUSILIERS
(11TH INDEPENDENT MACHINE GUN COMPANY),
CANADIAN ARMY

TRADE » MEDIC/STRETCHER BEARER

HOMETOWN » GILFORD, ONTARIO

Originally a member of the Royal Canadian Army Medical Corps, Albert Hogg transferred to the Princess Louise Fusiliers, an independent machine gun company of the 5th Canadian Armoured Division. He served with them in the Italian campaign, treating casualties of all nationalities as the unit's stretcher bearer.

I went to Avellino [Italy] from Africa. We went into the Princess Louise Fusiliers in 12th Brigade, an Independent Machine Gun Company. I was on my own—no doctors, just myself as a medic—and we had in the neighbourhood of 180 men in our platoons and groups.

We went up through Italy into the Hitler Line, the Gothic Line, the numerous lines that we had to pass through. One of these particular areas, the 88s [German anti-tank guns] were firing over the top of the soldiers ahead of us and landed in our particular campsite. I had a terrible, terrible experience. As a boy, as a young kid back in Canada, I watched the western movies. Anybody that got shot any-where, whether it be in the arm or the leg or the back, he was dead. Well, when these guys came up [for medical attention], they were still alive, but with their arms hanging off, or their legs crushed. I was bandaging up one fellow—he was in bad, bad shape. I finished putting all the bandages on him and preparing him for evacuation. I lifted him out of the stretcher and his back just literally fell out. He died right there in my arms. And that was only one of many people. It's in my mind all the time.

We had a young officer, a lieutenant who was in our group. And the lieutenant said, "Look, I'm going to try and get some sleep. I'm going to stay in that haystack. You guys know where I am." A shell came over. It didn't go off, but it went right through him and killed him. We had to dig him out behind the haystack and bury him in the field, just a shallow grave. Later, they'd take these people and put them in a proper grave in a different area.

Left: Young soldiers in 1940: Tom Reynold, Hogg, Reg Ball, and Reg Allman.
Right: Veterans in 2000: Reg Ball (deceased) replaced by Frank Poole.

Hogg was chosen for the honour guard when the Queen Mother inspected Canadian troops in 1942. Hogg is the eighth soldier in the first rank.

"I lifted him out of the stretcher and his back just literally fell out. He died right there in my arms... It's in my mind all the time."

I always felt that I was protected under the Geneva Convention of 1927. Nobody's going to shoot a medical man with a Red Cross on my helmet, a Red Cross on the back of my coat, my little bag of goodies. I had packages upon packages of morphine. I had all sorts of equipment to treat these fellows, right on the spot. I even had an opportunity to take care of a young girl who had picked up the detonator of a grenade and it had exploded in her hand. I took it to my officer and he said, "What can you do, doc, can you help her?" I had to remove two fingers from her hand and bandage her up—her hand was wrapped in a piece of ordinary brown paper because they did not have any method of treating her. The Germans took all the doctors and all the young men that they could possibly take with them as workers, so there was nobody left in the area.

That experience was very good. I left her with plenty of bandages and cream and sulpha [antibacterial medicine]. I never heard from her again, so I don't really know how she made out. But we often thought of her.

Top right: Hogg and his fiancée Lilian Jennings (married in June 1945), March 1945.

Above: During the Italian campaign, Hogg had to amputate two fingers from Maria's hand. Her grateful parents gave him this earlier picture.

Eric Jensen

BORN » KILLARNEY, MANITOBA
BRANCH » HMCS HAIDA, ROYAL CANADIAN NAVY
TRADE » COOK
HOMETOWN » NORTH YORK, ONTARIO

Many different components worked in harmony to help make the HMCS *Haida* the Royal Canadian Navy's most famous fighting ship. Of the more than two hundred officers and ratings onboard, however, few did more for crew cohesion than Eric Jensen, a cook who was "eager to cook."

I didn't want to be drafted by the army, so at seventeen-and-a-half, I went down to HMCS *York* [Toronto] to join the navy. I have marine life in my blood. My father, when he was a young man in World War I, joined the Danish merchant navy and had quite a time.

York was strictly a recruiting office. I was asked lots of questions and I had a physical. There were only three things they wanted people to do then, when they joined [in 1944]: to be a sick-bay attendant or a writer or a cook. I loved to eat, so I signed up to be a cook.

I got my cooking school down in Halifax after going to HMCS *Hunter* in Windsor [Ontario] for basic training. We had excellent instructors. They were chefs from Montreal, with many long years experience. They were wonderful. I can't remember how many hours a day we had instruction, but most of us were very sad when they'd say, "Well, that's all for today. We'll do some more tomorrow."

I got a draft for HMCS *Haida*, so that's where I went. There was 225 men, not counting the officers. I just did what I was trained to do. The only thing I didn't like, or had to get used to, was that if I was the first fellow on duty, the watchman would wake me up about six in the morning so I could get up, get up to the galley, and get the stoves fired up so we could make the breakfast for the day. I got over that very quickly because I really was eager to cook. I was enjoying every minute of it. There were three cooks and a baker, and a petty-officer cook was in charge of us.

When I got used to being woken up at six, I was the one that got breakfast going. And then another cook would join me. There were two cooks every time there was a meal, whether it was breakfast, lunch, or dinner. It took two of us to clean up the galley afterwards, because ev-

"We were like a family—brothers in arms, you always say. But everyone looked after everyone else."

erything we'd been using had to be cleaned spotless. We had a great big steam kettle—I can't remember the capacity anymore—but the last thing that was done with this steam kettle was to fill it up and make hot chocolate for the crewmen that had to work outside.

We got compliments every day. We had the best of everything. All the meat was down in the frozen locker. It was from Australia or New Zealand, all deboned and that. The supply officer used to have to bring this meat up when it was needed and it had to be up a good day beforehand, so it could thaw out. We had fresh potatoes; we had a lot of our own vegetables. Eventually they ran out and it was sometimes very hard to get something, like eggs and butter. Eventually, we couldn't get a hold of that, so we'd go to powdered stuff, powdered eggs and powdered potatoes and so forth. But the crew was happy with it. They always enjoyed it. We always got compliments. We were like a family—brothers in arms, you always say. Everyone looked after everyone else.

Above: HMCS *Haida*.

Jensen's medals: Arctic Star (left) and Soviet Sixtieth Anniversary of Victory in the Second World War Medal (right).

Glenn Price

BORN » MIDDLEVILLE, ONTARIO

BRANCH » THE HASTINGS AND PRINCE EDWARD REGIMENT, CANADIAN ARMY

TRADE » INFANTRYMAN

HOMETOWN » PETERBOROUGH, ONTARIO

Glenn Price celebrated his eighteenth birthday while en route to Europe in 1945. He joined the Hastings and Prince Edward Regiment in the Netherlands, taking part in some of the final battles of the war against Germany.

I joined up in 1944, and I celebrated my eighteenth birthday on the boat going overseas.

We couldn't wear our boots because there were German U-boats—submarines—in the area and the steel boots on the steel deck reverberated through the radar. So we had to go in our sock feet. When we got overseas, they threw the socks away, they were so dirty, and gave us new ones.

We landed in Liverpool and then went down to Sussex for some training. Then we went immediately over to Holland. We went to Nijmegen and we were sent up to the Hastings and Prince Edward Regiment. They were having heavy casualties in fighting the Germans and they needed replacements.

Our responsibility was to clear the Germans out of the Reichswald Forest. They were up in trees with high-powered rifles, killing officers, sharpshooting. We went through in Jeeps with flame-throwers on them and shot a flame-thrower up in the trees. They came down with their shirts on fire, I'll tell you. It was pretty gruesome, but we cleaned them out and took a lot of prisoners. We had to disarm them—take their pistols and rifles away—but they had no ammunition, it was all gone. They had no gasoline for their cars or tanks. They were all parked. All the officers had big Mercedes cars that they'd stolen from the wealthy Dutch people and they had no gas to run them. So Canadian officers took over those cars and ran them until the higher-ups said, no more gas for them cars. I had one for three days, but when I went to get gas they took it away. They were only for officers.

A lot of our fellows that I went overseas with were killed in that battle by those sharpshooters up in the trees. We showed no mercy when we got them down. We took

"I didn't understand German and they only knew a smattering of English, but we had conversations."

them prisoner and held them until after the war ended. Then we had to take them back to Germany by boat. We sailed from Nijmegen up to Bremen harbour, into the upper coast of Germany. There were six Canadians on each ship, and five hundred prisoners, and these prisoners all had squeeze boxes, accordions, and guitars—very musical lads. And there were six of us to raise the Canadian flag every morning and take it down at night and to guard these prisoners. But they were as happy as we were to see the end of the war. They were all our age too, just young kids really. They gave us no trouble whatsoever. I didn't understand German and they only knew a smattering of English, but we had conversations. They taught us some German songs and we taught them some Canadian songs and it was an interesting time.

Price's certificate of service, 1953. Price's discharge certificate, 1946. Soldier's service book, 1944.

Lawrence Wagg

BORN » SAINT JOHN, NEW BRUNSWICK
BRANCH » THE 8TH CANADIAN HUSSARS
(PRINCESS LOUISE'S); ROYAL CANADIAN ARMY SERVICE
CORPS
TRADE » DRIVER/MECHANIC
HOMETOWN » SAINT JOHN, NEW BRUNSWICK

Lawrence Wagg met his wife, Jean, a publican's daughter from Kent, while serving in England in 1942. His service also took him to North Africa, Italy, and Northwest Europe. While Ortona, "a horrible, horrible place to be in with the shelling," and Monte Cassino proved impossible to forget, it is the memory of meeting and marrying his wife that defined his Second World War experience.

We were in a place called Crowborough, which is just outside of Tunbridge Wells in Kent. I got a pass to go in to the city for the day. It was a Friday or Saturday, and I went to the dance hall there with a friend. We just looked around and came back out because he didn't dance and I'm not a dancer either. We were walking up the street and these two young ladies were walking down the street. We stopped and asked them where they were going. They were going up to the dance hall. We said, "No, it's no good tonight." So they, they took us up the street to this pub. We walked in, and there was the one girl's mother and fa-ther. She introduced me and we just sat and talked. When the time came for us to go, we left them, got in our truck and went back to camp. The next day, I went into town again. When I got to the pub, there she was. From then on in, she was my girlfriend.

In 1945, after I came back from Italy, I had my leave there and I asked her if she'd marry me. She said I'd have to ask her father. I asked her father in her presence if we could get engaged and get married. He said if she wanted to, we'd certainly have his permission. So we got an en-gagement ring, and I put it on her finger, and that was it.

Then we went over to France, and from France to Belgium, Holland, Germany and back out into Holland again. In 1945, I got a couple of weeks leave and went to England. We had a wartime wedding in a church, and while we were getting married, I was getting ready to go back over to Holland. But the big announcement came: the war had ended and all those who were on leave had an extra week or ten days. It was a wonderful thing.

"We had a wartime wedding in a church, and while we were getting married, I was getting ready to go back over to Holland."

Wagg and his wife Jean Patricia (née Craddack) on the day of their wedding, August 3, 1945.
Right: Winter 1940. Wagg is on the left.

Percy Jackson

BORN » LUCASVILLE, NOVA SCOTIA

BRANCH » THE NORTH NOVA SCOTIA HIGHLANDERS, CANADIAN ARMY

TRADE » INFANTRYMAN

HOMETOWN » BROSSARD, QUEBEC

One thing motivated Percy Jackson to join the army during the Second World War: the desire to be near his older brother, who was already in the service. Jackson succeeded in enlisting at age sixteen, although his age kept him out of action with the North Nova Scotia Highlanders in Northwest Europe. He finally caught up with his brother following the defeat of Germany.

I idolized my brother. He was my mentor, my hero. He was everything to me, he taught me everything. He was seven years older than me, and he went in the armed forces overseas. I was devastated. I was lost. I said, "I have to get in the army. I have to get in the forces, I have to get over there and either rescue my brother or follow my brother. And find him."

I tried to get in at fourteen, but the guy says, "I'm sorry, we have your birth certificate and you can't get in." I tried again at sixteen—walked in to Halifax recruiting and had no problem whatsoever. After the examinations and everything were over, they said, "Congratulations, you passed, you are now in the forces. Go back home for a couple weeks and we will call you. Get your business done." So I said, "I don't have any business to attend to." "You want to stay right now?" they asked. I said, "Yes."

I was a model soldier. My uniforms were pressed properly, my shoes were shined really good, and it was my discipline and my own respect that did this. My superiors recognized this and they made me a section leader within a month in the forces. That was in 1944. Then, just after Christmas, they said, "Well, now you're going overseas."

All I could think about, my mission, was to go find my brother. But I was supposed to be part of reinforcements for the North Nova Scotia Highlanders. I went up into Holland and I joined the unit. Then, all of a sudden, I was taken away. I found out afterwards that my mother had written a letter saying she knew I was in the forces and that I had no business there.

They took me from my unit and put me in a little ad-

"All I could think about, my mission, was to find my brother."

ministration tent. I said, "What am I doing here?" They said, "Never mind, just sit there." So I sit there and I sit there and I sit there. I said, "All my friends, my guys, my fellows I trained with, I'll never be able to find them, they'll be gone." I started to cry. They said, "Everything's going to be alright, but we found something wrong in your documents and we have to check and correct that."

They took me into Belgium, into an old army barracks where a lot of other soldiers were. I don't know what they were doing there just sitting around. They kept me there and they gave me jobs to do. I figured they'd found out my age.

May came, the war ended, and I was on my way back to my unit. I was looking for this person, looking for that person. I had a good friend, Gallant, from Prince Edward Island. I'm running around, looking for him. They said, "He was killed on the last day of the war." I blamed everybody for that. I blamed everybody. I said, "If I had been here, he wouldn't have been dead, you know?" I was crazy.

I got over that and I found my brother in Holland. I walked right up to him. He was down in a little pup tent [a small military tent] in an area in Goor. He was just pounding a peg in his little tent. He looked around at me, then took a couple more whacks, then looked around again. He was stunned. He said, "What the heck are you doing here?"

My mission was served for finding my brother. I really, really enjoyed being in the military. We were all the same: we dressed alike; we slept in the same quarters. And I retired at the end as a master warrant officer.

Left to right: Canadian Volunteer Service Medal; War Medal (1939–45); Peacekeeping Medal; United Nations Emergency Force (UNEF) Medal; United Nations Medal; Queen's Jubilee Medal.

André-Paul Turin

BORN » PARIS, FRANCE
BRANCH » ARMÉE DE L'AIR (FRENCH AIR FORCE)
TRADE » BOMBARDIER
HOMETOWN » PIERREFONDS, QUEBEC

Raised in Algeria, André-Paul Turin joined the French Air Force shortly after the Allies liberated the North African country in November 1942. While Turin was training as a navigator in the southern United States, the bishop of Quebec, who "had letters from young Canadian ladies who wanted to correspond with French soldiers," contacted the soldier's chaplain. Turin struck up a correspondence with a fellow francophone and his future wife, Marcelle Marier.

In spring 1944, I was sent from Tunisia to Casablanca, in Morocco, to await departure to the U.S. to train as a French aviator. I was French Cadet 4567. Craig Field, Alabama, was the landing base for all foreign aviators. There were aviators from China, Brazil, and from France. We each had our own specific training, hangars, dining halls, and we also learned English.

We also had a French chaplain. One day, he told us that he had received a letter from the bishop of Quebec. The bishop had letters from young Canadian ladies who wanted to correspond with French soldiers. I ended up corresponding with a woman who would become my future wife. Her name was Marcelle Marier. She was one of fourteen children and her father passed away a few days after we started our correspondence. Her family had to make it without their primary breadwinner and this was really hard for them, but we continued corresponding anyway.

We were given a little bit of American money to pay for our day-to-day living expenses and whatever other little whims, so I bought myself some stamps. It cost me next to nothing. Things were going alright, but later on I learned that my future wife didn't have much money. She had to borrow money from her elder sister and her friends to buy stamps. As we corresponded, we started growing on one another. I originally took an interest in her since when I was young, really young, I heard that people who corresponded during World War I made good marriages. This stuck with me and I said, well now, I have the chance to find someone serious since I have experience.

French fliers in training at Orangeburg, South Carolina, January 1945.

Victor Wong

BORN » VICTORIA, BRITISH COLUMBIA
BRANCH » FORCE 136,
BRITISH SPECIAL OPERATIONS EXECUTIVE
TRADE » SPECIAL FORCES
HOMETOWN » VICTORIA, BRITISH COLUMBIA

Like his fellow Chinese-Canadians, Victor Wong was denied the full rights of a British subject at the outbreak of the Second World War. Those rights were earned through the Chinese-Canadian contribution to victory over the Axis. Following enlistment in 1944, the British Special Operations Executive prepared Wong for service behind Japanese lines in Burma through extensive training in Canada and India.

Japan entered the war by bombing Pearl Harbor on December 7, 1941. By 1944, Japan occupied all of Britain's Asian territories. The British wired Canada and asked where they could find Chinese people who know English, and everything that is needed to help with guerrilla warfare. So the government sent letters to about eight thousand of us, to have us enlist. It was compulsory. Some of us wanted to go, and others were asking why we should go if we weren't even Canadian. In our town-hall meetings, we decided that the best way to do it was to sign up, go and come back and lobby for the franchise. And this is exactly what we did. Ninety-nine per cent of us joined general service, which means to go overseas.

I know a lot of Victoria [British Columbia] people tried to join and were turned away. Especially when they wanted to be in the navy. It was exactly like the British: they didn't allow anybody other than whites to join the navy. And the air force was the same. We weren't allowed to be pilots, but we could be air gunners. And they didn't want too many to join either. Only when Japan occupied all the territories over the Far East did the British want us to join in volume and do what they called Force 136 espionage work and organized guerrilla warfare. We were actually loaned to the British. We were under Lord Mountbatten and we were known as an SOE, which is Special Operations Executive, in SEAC, which is Southeast Asia Command.

We had a group of ten in different areas of training: communication, intelligence, language, engineering for showing how to build bridges. Also, to demolish them—the Japanese ones.

I want our people—the Chinese Canadians—to know that we went to war and returned. We won two wars: over Japan, Germany and Italy and freedom for Europe, and also freedom for China, because Japan surrendered. We came back and we lobbied the government, and in 1946, when we got discharged, Parliament passed the law saying that we can be Canadian citizens. It didn't became official until January 1, 1947, when Canadian citizenship came into effect.

"In our town-hall meetings, we decided that the best way to do it was to sign up, go, and come back and lobby for the franchise."

Top left: Wong (left) with his cousin Leonard Lee in Banff, Alberta, 1944.
Top right: Wong at Camp Shilo, 1944.
Left: Wong, Fred Yip and Dake Yip in Poona, India, 1944.

Joseph Gautreau

BORN » MONCTON, NEW BRUNSWICK

BRANCH » 1ST CANADIAN PARACHUTE BATTALION, CANADIAN ARMY

TRADE » PARATROOPER

HOMETOWN » DIEPPE, NEW BRUNSWICK

After training in the Maritimes and Newfoundland, New Brunswick native Joseph Gautreau dropped into Normandy with the 1st Canadian Parachute Battalion in the early morning hours of June 6, 1944.

For us, it [D-Day] was a real disaster. We had a lot of planes land one hundred miles away. They all got captured, prisoners of war. And we had a lot of casualties. A guy had the barrel of the machine gun, but no ammunition. Or the other fellow had the tripod, but he didn't have the gun. And I had the ammunition and I wasn't near where they were.

They showed us maps and the models of what the terrain was like where we were supposed to jump, but nothing works out that way. We'd seen all kinds of photographs, but they were taken when everything was dry. When we went, everything was flooded. People that landed in ditches drowned because their parachute dragged them right in the water. What looked like hedges on the picture turned out to be great big trees. Some got caught in the trees. We stopped at a guy who was caught, but he was unconscious. We all had a little bit of painkiller, a little needle we gave him, and we left him there and we took off. We couldn't wait for anybody else.

"I'm thinking, 'Holy geez, I just got here and the Germans are after me already.'"

On Christmas day, we went to Belgium by ship because the Germans had made a big push. Once we got over there, we slept in houses along the way until we got to the front. Near the front, we stayed in a little village in a school. The next morning, this little girl showed up and she says, "What are you doing in my school?" Now, she was talking French and I was the only guy who could speak French in that platoon, so I went over and I said, "Come on with me." I went down to the kitchen and gave her a big slice of homemade bread and put some jam on

it. The next morning we were packing when she showed up again. The kitchen was closing up so I gave her a whole loaf of bread and a can of jam. She said her dad wanted to see me. I went over [to her house]. He gave me a glass of wine, and we talked. After the war, my mother got a big envelope with a letter and the girl's picture on a card. I've still got that picture. In 1995, my two sons and I went over there and we found her. We took a hotel near her village for two nights. She said, "You've got to come here." I said, "No, we've got a hotel for two nights." "The third night, you've got to come here." So we went. She had a big spaghetti dinner and her children and her grandchildren were there. She was the most beautiful little girl you ever seen.

Top: Joe Campbell, Gautreau, and Ed Johnson, 1944.
Bottom: Madeleine Coppée, 11, whom Gautreau met in Belgium in 1945, and again in 1995.

Paul Dumaine

BORN » STE. HYACINTHE, QUEBEC
BRANCH » LES FUSILIERS MONT-ROYAL
TRADE » INFANTRYMAN
HOMETOWN » SAINTE-SOPHIE, QUEBEC

The attack on Dieppe made Paul Dumaine a German prisoner of war, but he endured the experience of captivity through the strength of his connection to his fiancée, Joan.

I have to tell you about this, because it wasn't all war—there was also love. I met a young woman, who I became engaged to. We didn't want to get married because the war was going strong and I could have been hurt or killed, so we said that we would wait until after the war.

One day, I left for Europe. On August 19, 1942, we arrived in Dieppe. My fiancée had no idea where I was. The battle was poorly organized. We lost everything we had to lose. I was injured and then taken prisoner.

Over there, the beaches are made up of little round pebbles. You walk and you roll. The tanks couldn't advance. The little stones would get caught in the tracks and they would break and remain stuck. All of the tanks were on the beach. A couple of them ventured into the city, but then they came back. Most of them were stuck on the beach. They could still shoot but they couldn't advance.

They had trouble getting messages out. The ships at large received a message that the city was occupied by the English-Canadian regiments, but that was wrong. Only a few men had advanced that far. They understood that the entire force was in the city. As it was occupied, they told the Fusiliers Mont-Royal, the reserve unit, to go in. They received the order to advance. We landed in broad daylight. We got there and the beach was ablaze. The battle was full-on. Everyone was getting killed and falling down all over the place. It was terrible.

I collapsed after an hour. My head was injured. I stayed a long time there just doing nothing. I couldn't walk. It was like I was paralyzed. I was bleeding and I wanted to get up. I wanted to go wash myself off in the ocean. I wanted to get up, but I couldn't. My legs were paralyzed from the shock of my injury. I had to drag myself on my elbows to the ocean. I washed my head with water. There was a great

big boat called a tank landing craft—a boat that carried tanks. The doors opened and the tanks came out.

One of them had foundered on the beach. It was there and it was burning. Just a bit of fire. We used it as a shelter to hide from the Germans. The injured went and sat at the back of the boat to avoid getting shot at. I went there right away. I had nothing left, no weapons. I stayed there for a while.

All of a sudden, I saw a German. He was an airman, and his plane had been shot down. He was making his way toward us on a little rubber raft. He arrived ashore and came toward me with his arms up yelling, "Kamerad! Kamerad!" He thought we were going to kill him. He came and sat beside me. He took some photos out of his pocket and he showed me his wife and children. He wanted to soften my heart so that we wouldn't kill him. He said, *"Fräulein, fräulein"* for his wife and *"kinder"* as he showed them to me. I didn't pay him any attention; I couldn't speak German. He stayed there until the end of the battle.

After three years as a prisoner of war, I was released. I was ill. When I got to England, I stayed in hospital for a month. Joan learned from others that I was in England. She was still in the army then—we weren't yet married. The colonel called her to his office and said, "Joan, I have some good news for you." She thought that it was news from her parents. "Your fiancée is in England, at Aldershot. I know that you would like to see him." She said, "Yes, yes, yes." "I am giving you a pass. Get dressed in civilian clothes and go see him." I was lying in my bed. They said to me, "Dumaine, you have a visitor." She was there. It had been three years. When I saw her, she was so beautiful. I took her in my arms.

When I got back in 1945, I married my wife. It was the most beautiful thing of the war. I suffered during the war, but my most beautiful memory was marrying her.

Left: Dumaine in Iceland, circa 1940–41.
Centre: Paul and Joan on their wedding day in England, July 4, 1945.
Right: Dumaine training in Peterborough, Ontario, 1940.

Blanche Lund

BORN » TORONTO, ONTARIO
BRANCH » WOMEN'S ROYAL CANADIAN NAVAL SERVICE
TRADE » DANCER IN THE MEET THE NAVY SHOW
HOMETOWN » BROOKSIDE, NOVA SCOTIA

Blanche Lund (née Harris) began dancing at a young age. She and her future husband, Alan, attracted the attention of Captain J.P. Connolly, a naval officer and impresario, while performing at a Montreal nightclub. Soon after, they had enlisted and were starring in the *Meet the Navy* revue.

I started dancing when I was seven years old. My parents didn't know where I got the idea from but I just said I had to dance and finally they gave in. My partner, Alan Lund, whom eventually I married, started dancing when he was eight. He did the same thing—bugged his parents until finally his mother gave him fifty cents and he went to the local teacher. She phoned and said he had a future in dancing, if he was interested. His mother was quite surprised because she didn't know he'd used the fifty cents for a lesson.

We teamed up when my husband was thirteen and I was fourteen. Eventually, we started going to Montreal, to some of the most terrible nightclubs. We felt that we could practise, and get the exposure, and that it would help us to become better. We built ourselves up to the point where we were playing nicer clubs. At this time, my husband was nineteen and I was twenty.

Captain Connolly was in charge of special services for the navy. I don't know how long he was in the navy when he decided he wanted to put a show together. Al and I were appearing at this nightclub in Montreal called Samovar, and he saw us dance. He invited us to come to his table, and when we sat down he said, "I have something to offer you." He told us all about this big show that he was putting together with a twenty-five-piece orchestra. It was going to play on the huge stages and it was going to have a huge cast. And he said, "Would you like to join?" We said we'd love to. And then he informed us that there was one catch: we had to join the navy. Being young, we both said, okay, that's fine.

Captain Connolly had great ambitions that the show would go to Broadway, and he did get an offer to take us

"When we opened in London, the front of the theatre was absolutely jet black."

down to New York. But the minister of national defence [for naval services], Angus Macdonald, said no way. He said if the show was going anywhere after Canada, it was going overseas. He said the show wasn't built for the American people; it was built for the Canadian servicemen and for the public, and to help build morale. We finally ended up on [HMCS] *Stadacona* in Halifax and had our shots and did our gas drill. And then we went overseas and arrived in Greenock, Scotland.

Our opening night in London was a very exciting time. When we had an opening night in Ottawa, it was like a Hollywood opening, with arc lights and all sorts of things. When we opened in London, the front of the theatre was absolutely jet black. People were lined up for blocks—the tickets had been sold for weeks before—but the lights and everything were inside the lobby. They couldn't show them because of the V1s and V2s.

When we were in London, we played two shows a day. We played so many shows a week just for the troops, and

On stage, London, England, February 1945.

"Al and I said, we're never going to separate, even to buy a sandwich, until after the war is over. So we didn't."

then we played shows for the civilians, but the troops could also come for free. There were two married couples in the show who were friends of Al's and mine. One was the girl who played the accordion with two men. The other girl was in the chorus and her husband was the rehearsal pianist for the show. Between shows one day, we girls decided to stay and make a pot of tea. We told the boys to go down to the café and get a sandwich for us so we didn't have to take our makeup off and put it on again.

So off they went. Marg got the teapot and she was heating the water and swirling it around the teapot and Billie, I don't know what she was doing, but at any rate, all of a sudden, this horrendous bang came and Billie was thrown out the door, I was thrown down on the floor with a chair on top of me and Marg was thrown on the floor still with the teapot in her hand. It turns out that a V1 had hit one of the barrage balloons that flew overhead and exploded in the air. And we thought, well, the boys are down at the café—it's probably been blown out. We

rushed down and met them at the middle of the road. My husband was on his knees in the middle of the road and Sid was on his back and Bill Richards was further up, way up the street, and all the windows in the café were blown out. Later on they told us what had happened. They said if the bomb had come down, we wouldn't be there. We were lucky those big balloons were put up to stop them. And so Al and I said, we're never going to separate, even to buy a sandwich, until after the war is over. So we didn't.

The show opened with sixteen sailors in white uniforms at the back of the set, which was built like a part of a ship. They were standing up there when the curtain opened, at ease. They all came to attention and marched straight down the stage to the footlights singing, "Meet the Navy and Greet the Navy, That's What We're Here For." It just took your breath away. The girls came on when they finished singing that first song, and they sang, "What's Weak About the Weaker Sex, What's Weak About the Girls." They did a number saying that girls were as important to the service as the men.

So we were doing the show and it was in the middle of the little "Chapeau" number, where the boys were in striped jackets and the girls were in bathing suits. The captain came onstage and put his hands out and everything stopped. "You'll all be happy to know," he said, "that it has just been announced that the war is now over." Well, you should have seen the audience! They came up onstage

and we all cried and everybody laughed. At that point, I think everybody pictured that they'd be going home right away. Of course, this didn't happen—it was many, many months before a lot of them got home. At any rate, after about half an hour of this screaming and yelling and carrying on, the captain came out and stopped everything again. He said, "Would you like the show to continue on, or do you want to all go?" Everybody said, "Continue, continue, continue!"

So we continued the show, but the people came up from the audience and joined in the numbers and so the show was absolutely a mess. But we all enjoyed it so much that we felt it was more fun than anything we'd ever done.

Top: With Noël Coward.

Bottom: The cast of the *Meet the Navy* show, circa 1943–45.

SERVICE

The war of popular memory is that of the infantry wading ashore at Juno Beach, ice-encrusted corvettes crashing through the churning ocean, and bombers rumbling over Germany as they sought to drop their payloads. Almost 1.1 million Canadians served in the forces. Although many never saw action at the front, they played no less of a key role in the Allied victory.

When Canada went to war on September 10, 1939, men and women enlisted from across the country and from all classes. There was no single reason. These young Canadians sought change, excitement, or a steady paycheque after years of economic misery. Some felt the pull of Empire or the need to respond to the rising threat of Hitler's odious regime—a regime that was intent on conquering Europe. Many Canadians believed that Canada had a role to play in stopping the Germans, and that waging war in Europe was preferable to fighting on the east coast or along the St. Lawrence River.

Shedding their civilian clothes and lives, the new recruits were prodded and studied by doctors and, later in the war, put through a battery of tests to identify their intelligence and suitability as soldiers, airmen, sailors, or one of the countless other trades. Unsure of themselves and the training they faced, the newly uniformed banded together, drawing strength from one another. The shared hardship of physical training and mental strain allowed many differences to melt away.

Women went through their own unique acclimatization and struggle. Some fifty-thousand served in the three services: the Royal Canadian Air Force (Women's Division), the Canadian Women's Army Corps, and the Women's Royal Canadian Naval Service. Their trades ranged from canteen workers to mechanics, from intelligence decryptors to cutting wood as "Lumber Jills," and many of these women later recounted proudly the important roles they played in supporting the forces at the sharp end. Despite their willingness to serve their country, women in uniform were often subjected to mean-spirited rumours about their

Pete Peterson

ARMED RECCE	1:45
PATROL	1:40
PATROL	1:25
ITEESCH & RHEINE	:30
PATROL	1:15
PATROL	1:50
PATROL	1:55
ARMED RECCE	2:00
RHEINE TO W1	:30
ARMED RECCE	1:30
ARMED RECCE	1:55
PATROL	1:10

2. L.B.S. 43   2 LBS
                B 5-6
THIS IS TO CERTIFY THAT—

No._____ Rank_____

HEISLER

Insert full name in capital letters and underline surname,
whose personal description, photograph and
signature appear hereon, is serving in the
_____

Changes in rank, or appointment to commissioned
rank are to be indicated below. All entries must be
made in ink by an officer. Signatures or initials are
not required.

New Rank	Effective Date	Reference of official authority for change in rank and date of authority
T/L/S	25/9/44	POR CAN 42/44
W/S	25/9/44	POR CAN 35/44

Personal description of holder

Height 5'9"   Build MEDIUM
Colour of eyes BROWN   Colour of hair BROWN
Date of birth 24 11 25

MLCC - 2S - 1945-46

CARD No. 161047

Signature of holder L. A. Heisler
Signature of issuing Officer _____
Rank S/O   Date 28.6.44

FLACK - K___
MAN   HIT
IN HUN ___

4 TRAINS DAMAGED
1 TRAIN DAMAGED   3 MET (1 DEST - 2 DAM)
F/L "JAKE" MAURICE   MISSING

EDLY RETURN - THE "OL" B JUST COULDN'T GO ANY FARTH
ARADO 234   DESTROYED (CONFIRMED)

OPS TIME   APRIL   36:35
TOTAL OPS   93:25

TRADESMEN'S QUALIFICATIONS
CANADIAN ARMY (ACTIVE)

This is to certify that

No. W-120846   Rank Private
Name Ruth Elizabeth HURLEY
was qualified in the Trade of Switchboard Operator "C"
                                    (Trade)   (Group)
and was employed at this trade in the CANADIAN WOMEN'S ARMY Corps
for a period of approximately Nine months.
The approximate civilian trade equivalent would be Switchboard Operator

Date 26 MAR 45
(DISTRICT DEPOT STAMP)   (Signature)
                                Jean H. MacFarlane Capt.
                                (M. Dorothy Bouchard) Major
                                O.C. #111 Depot C.W.A.C.
                                          (Rank)

MAR 26 1945
ROOM

xOfficer Commanding No. M.D. Eleven DxDx

NOTE:—Civilian trade equivalent will be assessed in accordance with Manual of Service
Trades and Civilian Equivalents (Canadian Army).

M.F.M. 423
50M—9-48 (7825)
H.Q. 1773-22-2200

low morality and lascivious behaviour, supposedly spurred by access to new incomes. It is hard to explain why the whispers ever gained traction. Clearly, the old prejudices about women working out of the home were resilient, even in the hyper-patriotic atmosphere of Canada in an unlimited war effort. While service women were hurt by these attacks, most were undeterred and took pride in their personal accomplishments and sacrifices. Full equality was never achieved, and most women went back to their homes after the war, but perhaps their successful wartime experiences, shared with their daughters, led that next generation to fight for more rights and equality.

The men and women who served their country behind the lines were the sinew that supported not only the war effort, but also Canadians in battle. Tens of thousands of Canadians also saw service in British formations, especially the Royal Air Force, Royal Navy, or British Army land units. And of course, after the war, there were veterans who immigrated to Canada from France, Poland, Britain, the United States, but also India, Africa, and Asia, who served in those national formations, units, and services. They, too, are veterans of the conflict, and perhaps reflective now of an ever-evolving Canada.

Behind: Pages from Brian MacConnell's Royal Canadian Air Force logbook showing enemy aircraft shot down, April 1945.
Top right: Glen Heisler's Royal Canadian Air Force identity card.
Bottom left: Ruth Hurley's tradesman's certificate as a switchboard operator in the Canadian Women's Army Corps.

Bob Farquharson

BORN » GLEICHEN, ALBERTA

BRANCH » NO. 435 (CHINTHE) SQUADRON, ROYAL CANADIAN AIR FORCE

TRADE » PILOT

HOMETOWN » TORONTO, ONTARIO

Air-dropping supplies was extremely dangerous work at any time, but particularly in Burma—while contending with the Japanese military, monsoons, and cumulonimbus clouds. As Bob Farquharson, a pilot with No. 435 Squadron of the Royal Canadian Air Force recounts, "We flew in everything that the army needed. Because it was the only way."

You know, there are no roads that join India to Burma. In fact, there were no roads at that time that joined any country to Burma. It was completely a mountain-locked country. There was one road—that was the one that went into China, called the Burma Road—but the Japanese controlled that. So there was no way to get supplies to the Allied army that was fighting the Japanese, except to fly them to them, so that's what we did.

To make a drop, you have to fly the aircraft "low and slow"—maybe three hundred feet above the ground. The kickers in the back piled the doorway with sacks of rice or whatever we were dropping. And we dropped absolute-ly everything. I've even dropped a crate of eggs packed in straw in a big wicker basket. Now mind you, eggs we always dropped with a parachute. And the gasoline we dropped with a parachute. But rice was free-dropped, called "slack packed-double sacked." It was packed slack, in a big hessian sack, and another sack over that, so it didn't burst immediately when it hit. In fact, it bounced and skipped along quite a ways before it came to rest.

We dropped absolutely everything. If somebody at the front had lost his eyeglasses or his false teeth, we flew in eyeglasses and false teeth. We flew in ammunition, cloth-ing, rations—all rations, petrol, barbed wire, spare parts for their vehicles. We flew in everything that the army needed. Because it was the only way.

The Air Force always tells you do not fly into a cumulo-nimbus cloud. They are usually about forty thousand feet tall and they're roiling inside with turbulence of up to one hundred miles an hour, winds of one hundred miles an hour, going up and down and everywhere. But, you know,

Top: The crew: Peter Wasylyshyn, Gordie Shellard, and Farquharson.
Bottom: Farquharson and his "basha" mates (Farquharson is centre top).

when the whole sky is full of cloud.... We used to say that meant it was ten-tenths cloud with intermingled mountaintops. There was just no way you could avoid it. I don't know of any pilot on a DC-3 on those runs who hasn't gotten into a cumulonimbus cloud whether you were supposed to or not.

I was caught in one. We were in cloud all around and all of it was looking pretty black, and what you'd do is just head for the lightest looking part of the sky that you could see and try to get ahead through that. Then you'd get into it and find it closing in behind you—just blackness ahead of you and blackness behind you. And so sooner or later you'd get into it. There's nothing you could do, nothing I could do, to change the position of the aircraft. It was going down, that's all there was to it. The climb and glide indicator was spinning around, the altimeter was just falling away, and we knew nothing but mountains was beneath us. We didn't know how far they were and down and down we went at about three thousand feet a minute.

"We dropped absolutely everything. If somebody at the front had lost his eyeglasses or his false teeth, we flew in eyeglasses and false teeth."

My second pilot and I—both of us with our feet on the dashboard and our hands on the wheel, pulling to try and pull the wheel back and get out of the dive—we couldn't move it. It was as though the controls were welded. And then all of a sudden it started going up again. We got into a bit of turbulence where it reversed and we were going up at the same rate. Finally, we broke through at the top and we could see little bits of lightness here and there. We headed for the lighter spot and finally got out. All the time we were in there, I was fighting it, you know, and I was determined that I was going to win over this villain that was out to get me. When we got out of it, my feet were shaking, my knees were shaking on the rudder pedals. I told the second pilot to take us home. That was the sort of experience that the monsoon clouds brought to everybody up there, when you had to fly no matter what.

Left (top): With Corporal White, USAAF, a Japanese fighter in south Burma.
Left (bottom): Ox carts picking up a delivery.

Earl Stiles

BORN » DORCHESTER, NEW BRUNSWICK

BRANCH » NO. 14 FIELD AMBULANCE,
ROYAL CANADIAN ARMY MEDICAL CORPS

TRADE » MEDICAL ASSISTANT

HOMETOWN » MADOC, ONTARIO

The official records refer to Earl Stiles as a medical assistant, but his comrades—as well as the German casualties cared for by the 3rd Canadian Infantry Division's No. 14 Field Ambulance—knew him better as a stretcher bearer. After landing in Normandy in June 1944, Stiles repeatedly witnessed the visceral consequences of war, including battlefield triage: "[W]hether it was a German there that's wounded and a Canadian wounded, who would you look after first? Well, depending who was hurt the worst."

In the army, when you're in action, it wasn't practical to carry whole blood in any way, shape or form. It has to be refrigerated and typed and everything. And so what they had in place of it was plasma. One bottle was a liquid—I suspect it was glucose—and the other bottle looked like... visualize cornflakes, smashed up into a powder like flour. And that's what it looked like. It was actually blood plasma. You could administer it to anybody, no matter what their blood type was. When we were in action, we had cases of this blood plasma. You'd take water in, pour it in with the blood plasma and shake it all up and you had the nearest thing to real whole blood that it was possible to have.

We'd have a casualty come into us, wounded. Just behind the front line, we could hook him up to this IV with blood plasma, hooked to the stretcher and a pole. In transit, he could be receiving this blood plasma. It was not as good as whole blood but it was better than nothing.

The worst thing I saw: I think the quadriplegic, both arms, both legs, I was summoned to look after. They brought him in on a stretcher. It was busy around there at the time, there was casualties coming and going and it was pretty hectic around the medical officers. They were busy. So I went over to this chap and, of course, there was no sign of life that I could see. I wondered if I could find a temporal pulse up in his head, because there's no way to check a pulse—his legs and arms are both gone. So finally after a few minutes, I go, "Hey, one of the docs, come over here." He looked for a few seconds and took off

and went to look after another casualty. And I wondered why he took off. So later on, after a hectic time, everything got a little quiet so you could breathe for a few minutes, I went to the medical officer and said, "Now what about that fellow." He says, "I couldn't find any signs of life." But what I was thinking, did I feel a temporal pulse or didn't I? We came to the conclusion that had we been able to save him, he wouldn't have thanked us, I don't think.

So that was probably the worst thing. The sixteen year old, he was interesting. It was shortly after D-Day, he was wounded in the leg or something and he could speak English. He was the only German that I handled. At that time, we knew that any German casualties were prisoners of war. They were coming back to England and eventually, they'd come into Canada. Canadians looked after them. We had camps set up around various parts of southern Ontario to house these German prisoners, either wounded or not wounded. So I said to him, "You're going somewhere I'd just love to go." And he said, "Where's that, where would

that be?" I said, "All of us will tell you, the war is over for you, you're going back to Canada and I'm going to Berlin." "Ha," he said, "you won't even get to Berlin." That made me mad. I said, "Listen"—because I knew they'd been indoctrinated with propaganda from the age of three, I imagine—I said, "Listen to this. I don't care if you believe me now, but remember, one year from today, we'll be in Berlin." I gave the stretcher a nudge and just got him the hell out of there.

"I've never seen such guts in my life, these soldiers. They had guts."

We looked after him, though, well. Now, you say, whether it was a German there that's wounded and a Canadian wounded, who would you look after first? Well, depending who was hurt the worst. And we were trained to do that. I don't know how they were trained but that's the way we were trained. So if the Canadian was wounded worst, we looked at him before the German. If he could hold his head up, to hell with you, I'd get there when I got there. But if he was hurt the worst, we probably would look after him. Most of the time, anyway, we'd do that.

I've never seen such guts in my life, these soldiers. They had guts.

Stiles, in England, 1943.

Betty Dimock

BORN » SAINT JOHN, NEW BRUNSWICK

BRANCH » SOUTH AFRICAN MILITARY NURSING SERVICE; ROYAL CANADIAN ARMY MEDICAL CORPS

TRADE » NURSING SISTER

HOMETOWN » WINNIPEG, MANITOBA

Betty Dimock (née Grimmer) realized her "great ambition" to serve as a nurse in the Second World War. In 1942, the South African military requested Canadian nurses to serve on loan. After a year treating wounded from the North Africa campaign, Dimock joined the Royal Canadian Army Medical Corps.

I was born in Saint John, New Brunswick, in 1916. Of course, that was during the First World War. I'm an identical twin. My mother and my sister and I were staying with my mother's parents during the war because my dad was overseas. He saw me when I was two weeks old and not again until I was four years old.

This was my great ambition—to be a nurse in the next war. There was a lot of talk about war at that time, so that was my ambition.

My first service, I was registered in the South African Army. It was with the South African Military Nursing Service. We were on loan from the Canadian Army to South Africa, accepting South African pay and discipline. The pay was very poor, about one-third of Canadian pay: the agreement was that we stay for one year.

Patients were from the North Africa campaign. You see, [German field marshal Erwin] Rommel was going through North Africa very fast, so they couldn't establish hospitals. There was a great call for hospitals to be established in South Africa, because that was the nearest Commonwealth country to the fighting. The wounded had treatment, but if they had lost a limb or were badly injured, they were just wrapped in plaster cast and shipped to us. So they were in very, very poor shape when they got to us.

Some of them never made the trip, of course. We had no antibiotics—it was before the days of antibiotics. Maggots did the work instead. And we had very few dressings. We had to wash out the dirty, old, soiled, infected dressings and hang them on the line in the sun and use them again that night. Native boys fanned flies off the wounds

Leaving New Brunswick for South Africa, April 28, 1942.

in the daytime, to try to prevent the maggots. And we had, of course, unfamiliar medication and treatment. It was quite a new experience.

One unforgettable case: a young English lad from the North African campaign with numerous injuries, in complete body cast, with maggots crawling out from under the cast in various locations. Removal of the cast exposed unexpectedly severe shoulder injuries. The area was filled with foul-smelling purulent substance, crawling with maggots. Apparently, he had had no care since leaving Egypt, three weeks prior to arriving at our place.

This patient begged me to get someone other than myself to perform the procedure. He was aware of what I would find. I needed a soup ladle to remove the pus and maggots. It was bad. And that, for a young nurse, was a little bit rough.

I didn't sign the second contract we got for the duration. It seemed to be a long way off at that time and I wanted to get into the Canadian Army, so I thought, this

UNION OF SOUTH AFRICA UNIE VAN SUID-AFRIKA

ACCREDITED REPRESENTATIVE
GEAKKREDITEERDE VERTEENWOORDIGER
OTTAWA
December 12th, 1941.

Miss E.E. Grimmer,
Laurentian Sanatorium,
Ste. Agathe des Monts, P. Q.

Dear Madam,

LETTER OF APPOINTMENT

You are hereby appointed as Nurse in the South African
Military Nursing Service subject to the following conditions:

(1) You agree to serve for not less than one year from the date
of your assuming duties at the hospital to which you are
allocated. At the conclusion of one year's service your
contract will end, but you will probably be given an opportunity
of renewing your contract for a further period.

(2) You agree not to resign for the purpose of marrying, or for any
other reason, without the approval of the South African Matron-
in-Chief, before you shall have completed your contract.

(3) For the purpose of routine and discipline, you will be subject
to the South African Military Nursing Service regulations.

according to South African rates, i.e., a S.A.M.N.S. Staff
is paid at the rate of £234 per annum, which at the present
rates works out to $1086.82. Certain of the Staff
may be selected at a later date by the Matron-in-Chief
South African Nursing Service for promotion to the rank of
in which case the pay will be £279 per annum which works
the present exchange rates to $1235.97.

- 2 -

class or best other available transportation will be
ded from place of enlistment to destination in South
a by the South African Government, and pay will commence
date of entrainment. On the completion of your contract
ar return transportation to Canada will be provided.

tfit allowance of $180 will be paid through the District
ster, Military District No.___, not more than three weeks
entrainment, and after one year's service, an outfit
allowance at the rate of one shilling per day will be paid.

(7) Disability pensions will be in accordance with the present
pension regulations for the South African Forces.

(8) You will be permitted to transmit any reasonable proportion
of your pay from South Africa to Canada.

Accredited Representative.

Miss E.E. Grimmer,
Dalhousie,
New Brunswick,
CANADA.

A.G. WAR RECORDS,
HAMILTON STREET,
PRETORIA.

Dear Sir/Madam,

You have provisionally qualified to receive the undermentioned awards, the
ribbons of which are attached hereto :—

OFFICIAL STAMP.

ADJUTANT GENERAL
HAMILTON STREET
29-5-1947
PRETORIA
WAR RECORDS

Adjutant-General.
Authority for Issue.

W.R. 308182/22

DEFENCE MEDAL BRITISH.
THE WAR MEDAL (1939/45).
AFRICA SERVICE MEDAL.

These awards are subject to final confirmation at a later date and subject to
forfeiture and/or restoration in terms of the British Army Council Instruction No.
A.C.I. 1452 of 31st. March, 1945.

Yours Faithfully,

R.G. Gibbings, Lt.
Col.

Officer in Charge, War Records.

THIS DOCUMENT IS NOT VALID UNLESS
IT BEARS THE OFFICIAL STAMP OF THE
ADJUTANT-GENERAL AND IS SIGNED BY
THE RESPONSIBLE OFFICER.

/ES.

"I needed a soup ladle to remove the pus and maggots."

is time for me to go home. It was very hard to leave these boys because they were really wonderful boys and accepting of the circumstances so easily, so well.

I arrived home I think it was August of 1943, and I immediately went in the Canadian Army. And then I went to England in the early spring of 1944. I was with a whole hospital unit, number 23. And I stayed with them until I left just before VE-Day, to go as reinforcement to number 1 Canadian General Hospital in Nijmegen, Holland.

When we went to England it was the first time we'd been associated with antibiotics, which was penicillin. And that was given every four hours, at least. Sometimes more frequently. And a big amount. Some of the needles were not too sharp when we had to shoot them into the boys. They just screamed, it was terrible. And they'd hide. That was a hard, hard treatment really for them, getting these shots of penicillin. And it was hard for us to do.

When I got back, I think the rationing was still on somewhat and it was a different life. Everybody had changed: civilians as well as military people. It was a war that put the women back to work. Prior to that, a married woman couldn't get any employment. And during the war, of course, they had to fill jobs that men left. So that's when family life changed completely. Mother wasn't home when the children came home from school because she was working. And that made a big difference. I grew up in a family where mother was always home. When we went in, the first thing we'd say was, "Mom, where are you?" And she always answered. Well, the children today don't experience that and that came from the war.

Opposite, clockwise: Letter of appointment to the South African Nursing Service, December 19, 1941; Dimock (right) and sister Martha Jean on leave in Paris, 1945.

Above: Defence Medal, Canadian Volunteer Service Medal, War Medal (1939–45), Africa Service Medal.

Jean-Marcel D'Aoust

BORN » ALFRED, ONTARIO

BRANCH » 6TH CANADIAN INFANTRY BRIGADE TRAINING
REGIMENT, CANADIAN ARMY

TRADE » INSTRUCTOR

HOMETOWN » BAIE-D'URFÉ, QUEBEC

Jean-Marcel D'Aoust "always loved being a teacher." That passion imbued his work as an officer instructing French-speaking infantry reinforcements for Les Fusiliers Mont-Royal—a regiment famous for its exploits at Dieppe, during the Normandy campaign, and throughout the liberation of the Netherlands—of the 6th Canadian Infantry Brigade.

At twenty-one years of age, one absolutely had to serve their country! I was brave, no more so than any others, but somewhat brave, so I enrolled and was invited to take a soldier and second-lieutenant course at camp Saint-Jérôme [Quebec].

After having received good grades at the camp, being the attentive student that I was, it was suggested that I become an officer, and I happily accepted; however, the leadership asked me to march with a group from Saint-Jérôme to Brockville, Ontario. It took us seven days and seven nights. Our goal was to take the Brockville military camp, which was mostly English-speaking, to prove to ourselves [we could do it] and to teach them what a military officer was, and would become.

After Brockville, I became a second lieutenant and I was sent to Farnham in the province of Quebec to qualify as a lieutenant, a full lieutenant. After several months of training, I was sent to England. In England, I was a lieutenant and [then] captain in the 6th CITRU Regiment [Canadian Infantry Brigade Training Regiment], in French it was called the Régiment canadien français de la 6e brigade. There, I became qualified to prepare the troops to suffer, and possibly die, on the beach at Dieppe.

As we all know, Dieppe was unsuccessful. But due to our experience at Dieppe, we learned a lot of things. This is what led us to win the war on the beaches of Normandy. I was the captain of the camp at Saint-Jérôme and this is where I showed soldiers who had enlisted voluntarily or who were called by the government how to walk with their heads held high, their hands low at their sides, looking straight ahead, and how to walk, left, right, left, right all

"If you aren't a good soldier, whether it is while working or at attention, you cannot win a war."

together. And it was these places that helped me become a captain and to be transferred to the military camp in Whitley, which was not far from London.

I always loved being a teacher. I liked showing others how to speak, what to say, how to walk, and how to be a soldier. If you aren't a good solider, whether it is while working or at attention, you cannot win a war. Fortunately, all of my soldiers were well trained and they really wanted to participate in a war which was well done. You know that, as a warrior, you have to want it. Maybe we were pushed; the government expects Canadians to serve during a war. But to go and fight against an enemy, it's this guy who decided, who was asked, and who accepted to go to the front line and fight the enemy. It was never forced, it was always voluntary, that each soldier responded to the call to invade Dieppe or to invade Normandy.

Top: Soldiers on the march in Saint-Jérôme, Quebec,1943.
Centre: A convoy of military vehicles, England, 1945.
Bottom: D'Aoust, with mechanical engineers, England, 1941.

Fred Linnington

BORN » SAINT-EUSTACHE, QUEBEC

BRANCH » SS NORFOLK, CANADIAN MERCHANT NAVY AND
HMCS STETTLER, ROYAL CANADIAN NAVY

TRADE » NAVIGATOR

HOMETOWN » SAINT-EUSTACHE, QUEBEC

An experienced lake freighter seaman, Fred Linnington worked aboard the SS *Norfolk*, a freighter that moved cargo between Canada, the United States, and the Caribbean. German U-boat activity remained a constant danger, especially in the waters around the Netherlands Antilles.

When the war came along, my good friend and I, we decided to find out what was going on. We went down to the harbour, and then up to the Canada Steamship Lines office. They had a ship called the *Norfolk*, which was sailing from Montreal in November of 1940 to go down to the islands. From the Gulf we had to go in and replenish the fuel to keep us going. We finally landed in Barbados, and that was the beginning.

From there, we went to different islands. Our main base was Trinidad. That was in the Gulf of Paria and there was one, two, three large ships ahead of us, anchored. And we were in this little small ship from Canada—a laker [lake freighter]. I was on watch at 11:00 and I heard, bang, bang.

And I saw the flame from the first ship. The second ship maybe five, ten minutes after, and about thirty minutes later, the three of them were all torpedoed. I got to the very end of my ship at the stern, so that I could get off, just in case we got hit. But they must have looked at us and said we're too small to waste a torpedo on.

In Dutch Guiana, we went up the Suriname. We finally docked our bow into the bank and a tug came around and towed us all the way up about five miles. It was during the night and you could hear the wild animals and you said, "God, we're really in the jungle." You'd be going along and there would be foliage breaking and landing on the ship. And my worst fear was that a snake would fall onto the boat. That was one thing I was always worried about.

The most impressive thing was the natives—they'd never seen us, you know, members of a ship. They were there and they were looking, begging for different things. Well, I knew I had a winter jacket, a beautiful jacket. I traded it for something that I wanted and they had. That

worked out well. And they were looking for something to drink. And I had some ice and they didn't know what ice was. I gave it to them and they thought it was fire. And I showed them what I was doing, eating it. And then once they got to know what it was and it tasted good, they were asking for more. It was beautiful cruising down there.

There were a lot of submarines in the Caribbean in that time of war. A lot of ships, especially down there for oil, were torpedoed. They used to go into Curaçao, that's a Dutch island down there, and there's a big place where you could take a ship in there, dry dock, and they would repair those that could be repaired and get them back to sea.

We had a great trip back home. We were dropping in at all the different islands all the way down to New Orleans, going up into the Mississippi. A day before we got into that area, we stopped dead. Everyone said, no smoking, nothing, no lights or anything outside. We had to watch what we're doing because they [the Germans] had a guard on there and if anyone had lit up a cigarette, they would have been shot dead right away. It was so dangerous around there. They were sinking ships because they were going in there to get cargo to take over to Europe. The submarines were out there in the big bay. It was good for them, and the navy wasn't in there taking care of it like they could be, because they were so stressed for ships.

I eventually got back to Montreal and that's when I joined the Royal Canadian Navy. I had a great position. I knew where we were going and what we were doing before anybody else. I used to get the information from the navigator. I used to check the charts and do all the corrections, bring it all up to date.

Off the Bay of Biscay, we got in a signal that the war was over. We had eight big troop ships, and we put on the lights—they lit up all the ships and everything else and we went up there with the siren. And they were blowing their horns and everything. That was the greatest thing.

1939–45 Star; France and Germany Star; Canadian Volunteer Service Medal; War Medal (1939–45).

Hubert "Dodd" Gray

BORN » MONTREAL, QUEBEC
BRANCH » NO. 40 SQUADRON, ROYAL AIR FORCE
TRADE » WIRELESS AIR GUNNER
HOMETOWN » MONTREAL, QUEBEC

Dodd Gray was one of the relatively few Canadians who served in the North Africa campaign. He and his multinational comrades in No. 40 Squadron of the Royal Air Force conducted bombing raids against the Italian and German forces and endured service life in one the most inhospitable climates on earth.

We were on 40 Squadron, attached to the Royal Air Force [RAF] out in Egypt. Our crew was Australians, New Zealanders, English, and Canadians. We were the ones that kicked Rommel up to Tripoli.

We lived mainly in the desert. It wasn't very pleasant, either, especially if you got into a sandstorm. Then you just stayed in that tent because you couldn't even breathe outside. You can't eat or cook because everything goes in your food. At night, you'd have a leather plastic sheet or something. We made a hole in the sand for our hips. You got used to it. When you spend a year there, in all that heat, you sort of learn a few things.

The temperature some days, it was up in the nineties, but it was a dry heat, very dry. We used to wander. We'd meet the odd Bedouins with their camels. We had to be careful. In Egypt, I always carried a pistol on my hip—we had to, but generally, they didn't bother us too much.

Once we were in the desert, over Tobruk [Libya], and there were fifteen aircraft waiting for us to go in and light up a target. We went in at about twelve thousand feet with all the flares. Going in was quiet, but as soon as we got into the middle of the target, the massive searchlights picked us up and we were caught. We had already dropped our flares, so we just put the nose down—almost ninety degrees—and went straight down to get out of the searchlights.

When we dove and then pulled out, our instruments sort of went haywire. Coming out to the target, the Mediterranean is usually on my right, and going back it's supposed to be on my left. So I'm sitting there wondering, what's the Mediterranean doing on my right again? So

"[I]f you got into a sandstorm...you just stayed in that tent because you couldn't even breathe outside. You can't eat or cook because everything goes in your food."

I said, "Hey Skipper, how come the Med's on my right? Shouldn't it be on my left? We're going home?" He says, "Let me check it out, Dodd." And sure enough, our compass was all mixed up. And the guy says, "Thanks, Dodd, now you can go to sleep."

We turned around and went back. And then he said, "Now look, guys. We may not have enough gas. We may have to land in the desert, so let's get the aircraft ready." That's just one of the things that happened.

Gray and his crewmates in North Africa, circa 1941–42.

Giles Doucet

BORN » BATHURST, NEW BRUNSWICK
DECEASED » MONCTON, NEW BRUNSWICK (2009)
BRANCH » MV ASBJORN, DANISH MERCHANT NAVY
TRADE » COOK
HOMETOWN » MONCTON, NEW BRUNSWICK

Giles Doucet joined the merchant navy as a cook at sixteen years of age. His first voyage, in the Danish ship MV *Asbjorn*, involved transporting ordnance from Halifax to Britain while under attack by a wolf pack of German U-boats.

I was a cook. I started as galley boy and worked myself up to assistant cook, then second cook, and eventually to chief cook. It was very interesting, but in those days, we ate a lot of powdered eggs and dried potatoes and powdered milk. In England, the stores weren't very good because we only bought the same thing. So we had good food when we were in Canada or sailing out of Canadian or American ports.

We took a full load of high explosives from the magazine in Bedford Basin [Nova Scotia]. We sailed out of there in early November [1942]. Everything was great until about three days out, when we ran into a wolf pack of submarines. That was my first action. The captain of that ship was Danish—the whole crew was Danish except for two Canadians,

myself and an able seaman—and when the ship was being torpedoed, the captain asked permission from the commodore to leave the convoy on its own, because we were very fast and could outrun any submarine. But the commodore denied him permission. I can still remember him saying, "*Fones te hell*," in Danish, which means "the devil's in hell with you." "You give me a destroyer and a smokescreen— let me out of this predicament," he said, "because I've got a cargo here that'll blow you and your whole convoy apart." So the commodore, hearing this, allowed them to lay down a smokescreen and we took off for ourselves.

I can remember being very, very scared. There was an old boatswain there and he noticed how scared I was. He told me, "You come up with me. After this is over I'll give you something to straighten you out, to calm your nerves." He took me up to his cabin and he poured me out a tumbler full of this Saint-Pierre [and] Miquelon rum. We landed in Liverpool, England, about five or six days later and discharged this cargo.

"It was very interesting, but in those days, we ate a lot of powdered eggs and dried potatoes and powdered milk."

We were great buddies aboard ship. Everybody looked after everybody else. If you forgot your life jacket, there was always somebody there to make sure he ran for your life jacket in the galley or in your cabin, wherever you happened to have it. And he would always be watching your back.

Top: After the war, Doucet wore this merchant navy badge on the pocket of his blazer.

Centre: After the war, Doucet wore this beret as part of the Merchant Navy Veterans' Association on Remembrance Day and at other commemorative events.

Bottom: Doucet's service medals left to right: 1939–45 Star, Atlantic Star, War Medal (1939–1945), Queen's Jubilee Medal, and Canadian Volunteer Service Medal.

Clinton Hayward

BORN » HARTLAND, NEW BRUNSWICK

BRANCH » GROUND CREW, NO. 427 (LION) SQUADRON, ROYAL CANADIAN AIR FORCE

TRADE » BOMBSIGHT INSTALLATION AND MAINTENANCE

HOMETOWN » MIRAMICHI, NEW BRUNSWICK

Clinton Hayward served as an "erk," one of the ground crew personnel who ensured that the pilots and bomber crew of the Royal Canadian Air Force (RCAF) went into action with the best-maintained equipment possible.

They took us by bus at night to New York and got us off at 22nd Street. We marched down to the [RMS] *Aquitainia* and they put us on the lower D deck, because the top decks were all filled with American Army troops. We sailed from New York in the morning and the last thing I saw was the Statue of Liberty standing in the harbour.

We landed in Greenock, Scotland, and they took us over to the pier in a smaller boat. We got off the pier and were standing there, waiting for a train. A seagull went over us and let it go, and it hit a fellow next to me. He had white scum all down his nose and his cap. And he said, "That's a poor sign." I said, "Why?" He said, "It's a sign I'm not going to make it back." And he didn't.

We went to Bournemouth as soon as we landed in England—that's where all the recruits went. They sent me to Leeming, Yorkshire—a heavy bomber squadron. At that time, we were flying [Handley Page] Halifaxes. They were four-engine bombers, comparable to the [Avro] Lancaster [Bomber], but the Lancaster was a better ship. The Halifax would carry around twelve thousand pounds of bombs, where the Lancaster—we got that just before the end of the European war—would carry fifteen thousand to twenty-two thousand pounds of bombs. That was a lot of bombs to let go.

When I was there about three weeks, they sent me to Manchester where they were making the bomb-aimer's instrument; they call it the Mark 14 Jarrow bombsight. I was a specialist on that. I had to check all the 427 Squadron bombsights, whenever the missions were finished, to make sure they worked well. A little cord ran from the bombsight over to the side of the plane, and when you were coming in to bomb, the bomb aimer was in charge of the plane—telling the pilot to go left or turn right. The bombsight was always level with the earth, so the plane could dip any way and you'd still be on target. It was a very secret bombsight, and the big factory where they made them was secret.

I went to London on leave one time by myself and that's when the V2s were going over. I was walking back to the YMCA and one went off quite near where I was walking. I never even heard the explosion. All I know was that I was in the air, going backwards. All the buildings in London then were bombed out, and just had the cellars and basements left, they always built a wooden fence around them. I hit this wooden fence and a big piece of it broke off and I just spun around and landed about thirty feet down in a cellar. Wasn't even scratched. I didn't know how the devil I was ever going to get out—I'd have to wait until morning. Then somebody up top hollered, "Are you alright?" And I said, "I think so." He said, "Well, I'll throw a rope down.

"He dusted off my shoulders and I had the Canadian patch on my arm. He said, 'I might have known. Canadians are hard to kill.'"

Do you know how to tie it?" I said yes, so he threw it down and I tied it around me and he pulled me up.

When I got up there, I saw it was a bobby. They were policemen and they had to be six feet and they had to weigh a certain amount before they'd even take them. He pulled me up just like he'd pull up a fish. I had a lot of dust and everything on me. He dusted off my shoulders and I had the Canadian patch on my arm. He said, "I might have known. Canadians are hard to kill."

No. 427 (Lion) Squadron, RCAF, with a Lancaster Bomber, at end of war with Germany.

Ray Lewis

BORN » ATHABASCA, ALBERTA

BRANCH » THE WESTMINSTER REGIMENT (MOTOR),
CANADIAN ARMY

TRADE » DRIVER/MECHANIC

HOMETOWN » ST. ALBERT, ALBERTA

Ray Lewis was originally trained as a driver/mechanic rather than a combat soldier, but he served in Italy—where he was wounded in action—and Northwest Europe as a Bren gun–carrier crewman in the Westminster Regiment.

I tried to join the army on two occasions prior to getting in, but I was found out to be too young and rejected. Finally, I got in when I was seventeen. It was October. I wouldn't be eighteen until January, so I really didn't have any place to go. I had no training. I was the orderly room runner. You rode a bicycle and posted the daily orders in various messes and those kinds of places. And then I think my father, who was the quartermaster sergeant in Calgary, must have arranged a driving test. I passed that without any trouble and two weeks later, I was instructing in driving. My first batch of candidates were senior officers. That's pretty much what I did. I was sent off to Italy because the Westminster Regiment, which was motorized, needed people with my qualifications—driver/mechanic.

I was sent to the regiment on about the twenty-fourth of May 1944, right after the Melfa crossing. I'd never had a rifle in my hand; I'd never fired a rifle. They give me a Bren gun with the Bren gun carrier. I had to learn to drive a Bren gun carrier. We had a thirty-calibre machine gun mounted on the front of the carrier and a PIAT [projector, infantry, anti-tank] gun, which was an anti-tank weapon. I'd never handled any of these things before, ever. I went to the regiment in May because the guy who was doing that job got killed. And then when I was wounded, another fellow took my place, and he got killed. Another fellow took his place, and he got killed.

I went back to the regiment with one of my wounds still seeping. I had to change the bandage on it myself. The 5th Division, which I was in, and the 1st Division, which was also in Italy, then joined the other Canadian divisions. It was a whole Canadian Army and we wound up in the little town of Delfzijl in northern Holland, about as far north as you can get.

"I was overseas for two years less six weeks. I was back in Canada before I was twenty-one. Legally, I couldn't vote or buy liquor."

The Germans were using up all the ammunition they had. They had their back to the sea, no place to go. A friend of mine, Gould, he and I had signed up to go to the Pacific, because we knew the war in Europe was winding down. One day, we went up to this elevated railroad track. We looked over and we could see a German tank, maybe five hundred yards away. Just as we looked, we saw a puff of smoke. We went down immediately, almost at the same time as a shell hit maybe twenty feet away, on the other side of that railroad track. We went back and took our names off the list to go to the Pacific.

I was overseas for two years less six weeks. I was back in Canada before I was twenty-one. Legally, I couldn't vote or buy liquor.

Top: Lewis and a friend the evening they enlisted. Calgary, Alberta, October 22, 1942.
Bottom left: Telegram dated October 2, 1944, related to Lewis' wound during the Italian Campaign.
Bottom right: Lewis and his sister on the morning he enlisted. Calgary, Alberta. October 22, 1942.

Bob Govan

BORN » SASKATOON, SASKATCHEWAN

BRANCH » 2ND HEAVY ANTI-AIRCRAFT (MOBILE) REGIMENT, CANADIAN ARMY

TRADE » ARTILLERY FUSE SETTER/GUNNER

HOMETOWN » QUILL LAKE, SASKATCHEWAN

Bob Govan set the fuses for and helped crew 3.7-inch heavy anti-aircraft guns, among the most powerful Allied artillery used in the war. His unit defended Britain from German bombers and V-rockets and supported the Allies throughout the Normandy and Northwest Europe campaigns.

When you went on the guns on "Doodlebug Alley" [in South London], you went on for twenty-four hours at a time. We went because these men were playing out. The raids usually started about 5:30 in the evening, and they came over mostly from 6:00 until about 8:00. Not too many during the night, but some. They were all VIs. They had a motor that shot flame out the back, so you could see them quite plainly. We weren't allowed to go into air-raid shelters. That was for civilians. They had trenches dug around in different cities and places, but we weren't supposed to go in.

We had to go across the English Channel to get to France, and they were shooting from Cap Gris-Nez across to England. They would also shoot at the ships going down the Channel until the Allies put up so much of a smokescreen that they couldn't see where we were. We landed with landing craft because the boats couldn't get in close to shore, but the fighting was back far enough so that there were no problems for us.

We moved up to Falaise. From Falaise, we went up to places like Boulogne, Calais, and all up the west coast of France. I was called a fuse setter. I'd prepare the shells for firing and I'd set fuses. When I wasn't setting fuses, quite often I was loading the guns. We fired nearly all air bursters. We tried to burst them in the air, just above the ground a little bit, so they would spread out. I spent three years on one gun, so I got to know what it was like. That was a [QF] 3.7 [inch AA] gun. It's just called a 3.7.

Our extreme range was fourteen miles, and it took nine men for a crew. We had 275 shovels. You dug your gun in, then you dug your slit trench alongside, then you went back a little bit behind and dug a hole to sleep. You tried to

"It's the loudest thunder you ever heard. And when it quit, you never heard anything so quiet. Nobody talked, they just sat down."

cover it up with planks and some dirt. Usually it was a door off of some poor farmer's house that went over the top.

Sometimes, at night, we used to fire on what we called a "time on" target so the infantry could try to get some sleep. Our whole line would just fire one shell, then wait maybe half an hour and fire one more, just to keep them on edge on the other side. You might be firing every gun in a twenty-five-mile line, exactly at the same time.

It's the loudest thunder you ever heard. And when it quit, you never heard anything so quiet. Nobody talked, they just sat down. You know, the pressure's great, and when that pressure was off, well, you just sat down; you didn't even talk amongst yourselves. And for two days after, we slept. No celebration or anything. When it quits and the guns stop firing, you're not enemies anymore.

Top: Govan (third from right) stacking ammunition near Dunkirk, France, January 20, 1945.
Centre: Preparing to move a 3.7-inch gun, Belgium, 1945.
Bottom: 3.7-inch gun, Germany, March 1945.

Fred Chapman

BORN » REGINA, SASKATCHEWAN

BRANCH » ROYAL CANADIAN ARMY PAY CORPS

TRADE » PAYMASTER

HOMETOWN » EDMONTON, ALBERTA

Fred Chapman played a key role in the Canadian Army: he made sure his comrades received their pay. Never far from the front lines, especially in actions such as the Sicily landing, Chapman handled numerous currencies and endured enemy artillery shelling and air attacks.

I was in the Sicilian invasion but I didn't land with the first wave. The first landing was on July 10, 1943. I landed with my group on July 13, three days after. During that night, the German aircraft came over. They were bombing and strafing us and we were wide open on the beaches. At that time, I was a warrant officer, even though I was only twenty-two. I was in charge of the men under me and I had to get them off the beach, into a place that was at least sheltered a little bit by one of those rock fences that they are so familiar with over there. I went to get up, but I was frozen stiff, couldn't move. It lasted for maybe a few seconds. I told myself, "You've got to get up and get over here, get those guys over." It couldn't have been very long, maybe only a few seconds, but it felt like an eternity with the bombs and machine guns firing and all that sort of stuff.

Eventually, I just jumped up on my feet and I said, "Come on, you rotten dirty buggers, get over here." And they all moved. And that was my baptism of fire. That was one incident that I never forgot, and I was scared to death.

I was with the 1st Canadian Infantry Division and we were right at their headquarters. We'd take charge of anything that came up in connection with pay, particularly when the soldiers wanted to go on leave or when they needed a little money for something or other. There's a paymaster for every regiment and a field cashier who was with the division, who services all these regimental paymasters. We looked after a lot of things, not just the pay. Some of the soldiers liked to send money home to their wives or sweethearts or whatever. That was all done for them by us at no charge, and we did a lot of other things connected with their uniforms and that sort of stuff.

We were there right with the division. We sat at a table

under a tent with our rifles right beside us because if the headquarters happened to be overrun, then we got out and fought like everybody else. So we were there. We weren't normally engaged directly with the enemy, but the soldiers that were marched right past our tents. They were on either side of the road, in formations. We were right there. We got shot at like everybody else, and we got strafed and bombed and suffered artillery fire and all that sort of thing.

We were watchful all the time. I was in one spot where these German aircraft—what was called a Focke-Wulf—came over. A Focke-Wulf was a fighter bomber and a better aircraft than the Messerschmitt. We had an aircraft signal and this went off when I was doing something, I forget what it was, near one of the camps. I heard this aircraft come over and it came right straight down to me. And I went flat on the ground. The way the trees and the

Above, left to right: Two unknown, Charles Shattick, Captain Mitchell, and Fred Chapman, Holland, 1944.
Right: Chapman at Aldershot, England, 1941.

foliage were, he couldn't stay; he had to zoom and sort of veer off to the right. I saw these bullets just tearing up the ground right in front of me. It was a very scary thing. How I came through it without getting a scratch, I'll never know, but I guess the good Lord was looking after me at that time.

I was the warrant officer, but we had officers too, a major and a captain. And they were responsible for looking after the actual cash because you had to be careful. We had what we called British Military Authority—the facsimiles of the pound and shilling. It wasn't actual currency, but it was a valid for issuance to the soldiers and they could go to the town.

The local people in Italy were willing to accept it. The payoff, of course, was that we carried a number of currencies. There was American currency, there was English currency, French currency, Belgian francs, Dutch guilders, and this sort of thing. Everywhere we went, we picked up the currency from the local banks.

John Zacharias

BORN » HERBERT, SASKATCHEWAN

BRANCH » ROYAL CANADIAN ORDNANCE CORPS

TRADE » ORDNANCE SHIPMENT AND DISPOSAL

HOMETOWN » VICTORIA, BRITISH COLUMBIA

An expert in the safe movement and disposal of munitions, John Zacharias and his Ordnance Corps comrades supported training operations and the joint Canada-U.S. liberation of the Aleutian Islands.

I had to learn about all the munitions. There are small arms, grenades, explosives of all kinds, artillery shells, mortars, and so forth. I had to learn all about all of those. We supplied all the training units in Pacific Command with munitions, whenever they wanted them. And there were some artillery camps on the coast for the defence of Canada; we supplied them with ammunition, too.

Mortars were quite different from artillery shells, in that they were used over a relatively short distance. The troops would fire a mortar off against the enemy, but they were close enough for these to have some effect. On the other hand, the artillery shells were for long distance. Grenades were used when soldiers were fighting the enemy at a relatively short range, where you could just throw a grenade over and it would explode. It was all very deadly stuff that we were dealing with, but I hope it did some good to the fellows in training to go overseas.

The office of the ammunition dump would give us the orders from various army units in training in B.C., and we would have to ship them whatever we had and what they wanted. When they finished their training and went overseas, they would send all their remaining munitions back to us and I had to check them to make sure they were still okay. If they weren't, I had to blow them up.

I wasn't as careful as I should have been and I didn't wear anything over my ears when I was doing that, so I ended up being deaf in one ear. I'd have to tape some explosives to the shell I was blowing up and then have a fuse, which I could light after I got out of the way. Eventually, the shell or whatever it was would blow up.

There was one time when the Japanese had occupied the island of Kiska, which is in the Aleutian islands off Alaska, and we had to supply the Canadian Army going

up there with all sorts of explosives and munitions. Most of it was never used because the Japanese fled. It came back in terrible condition. It had been sitting out in the weather and we had to go over it all and dispose of what we didn't think was usable anymore.

"It was all very deadly stuff that we were dealing with, but I hope it did some good to the fellows in training to go overseas."

Top: Zacharias, March 2010.
Bottom: Zacharias on leave in Calgary, Alberta, 1943.

Helen Jean Crawley

BORN » LONDON, ENGLAND

DECEASED » MISSISSAUGA, ONTARIO (2010)

BRANCH » 93RD SEARCHLIGHT REGIMENT, WOMEN'S AUXILIARY TERRITORIAL SERVICE

TRADE » SEARCHLIGHT OPERATOR; DISPATCH RIDER

HOMETOWN » MISSISSAUGA, ONTARIO

Helen Jean Crawley joined the Auxiliary Territorial Service in 1942, one of more than 190,000 British women who did so during the Second World War. She operated searchlights scanning the British skies for German bombers and later volunteered as a dispatch rider on a Norton motorcycle.

A lot of people want to call them spotlights, but they're not spotlights—they're searchlights, because you search the skies with them. And when the Number 7 [operator] threw the switch, the light would come on, and that was twelve thousand candle power. At the back of the searchlight, there used to be tarpaulin sheet and two seats, and you'd have like a little television set in front of you. It was called a cathode ray tube and there was a line across it with a V in the middle and when we were searching, if a dot came in the V, you'd shout out, "On target!" And she'd throw the switch and hopefully light up a plane so that the Royal Artillery could shoot it down.

We never used to get undressed at night. We just used to take our boots off and lie on the bed, because when you had to stand to, which meant enemy planes were on the way, you had to get on the equipment and you had fifteen seconds to do it. We just put our boots on and that was it. Sometimes we were out on that equipment until three or four o'clock in the morning. And we would be singing all sorts of songs—you know, "Show me the way to go home" and things like that—to keep awake. We would manage to get maybe a couple hours of sleep, then we had to get up and do the maintenance on the equipment, which had to be done every day, whether you'd slept or not.

When the bombing stopped, they didn't know quite what to do with us. The letter came around asking for volunteer dispatch riders, so I thought, oh, I'll be a biker. They sent me to North Wales to do motorcycle training. The men didn't like us at all. They used to take us up these roads where it was all loose gravel and they would come along beside us and push us off the bike. Or they would throw the bike on the ground and you had to lift it up; I

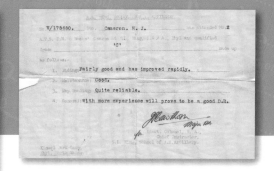

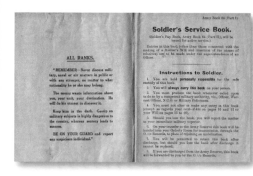

One of the searchlights used by the 93rd Searchlight Regiment.
Ginger Noakes is standing on the searchlight.

Officer inspecting the 93rd Searchlight Regiment, 1943.

*"We had to put up with a lot from the men,
and yet without us, as Mr. Winston Churchill said,
'without the women, we may have lost the war.'"*

remember once my anger took over, and I got down and picked the bike up and stood on it, and I was gone.

They gave us these big boots and great long overcoats and crash helmets and big gloves, and with the grime and that on the roads, you looked dreadful. One day, I thought, I'll call in the Union Jack Club and have a cup of tea. So I walked in there with all this on and ordered the tea, and then I went to the ladies room. Every girl in the army reserved this pocket on the left hand side of the jacket for powder, comb, and lipstick. I went into the ladies room, took off my crash helmet and made myself look halfway decent. And then I went out to have my tea. There were six or seven soldiers in there and within a couple of minutes I had three or four of them sitting at my table. I was a good-looking blond in those days! They just didn't know it was a girl, you see, with the crash helmet on.

We had to put up with a lot from the men and yet without us, as Mr. Winston Churchill said, "without the women, we may have lost the war."

Top: Crawley and her friend Rose Eagle, 1944.
Bottom: Crawley on a Norton motorcycle, 2005.

SURVIVAL

The difference between victory and defeat on the battlefield, and ultimately in war, is which side can hold out longer. What can a people stand as they face economic privation, unrelenting losses, or even starvation? What can the soldiers endure as they confront untold hardship, unimaginable mental and physical strain, and the myriad factors that affect their chances of perseverance?

The battlefield is a place of brutality. Soldiers, sailors, airmen, tankers, engineers, and all other combatants face dismemberment and death. How do they survive the mental strains at the front? All have their breaking point. Duty and empire, gallantry and heroics; these ideas seem to dissolve under the strain of war. Warriors know and often care only about survival. It is kill or be killed.

In battle, soldiers, sailors, and airmen survive from good training. Sometimes that is not enough. Combat experience brings a sixth sense of knowing when to drop into a smoking shell crater and when to run full bore. But on a battlefield of whirling metal, even the bravest and best died.

Efficiently crewed ships were hit by torpedoes and bombers were torn apart by night fighters or flak fire, despite the crews' best efforts or accumulated battle experience.

Remarkably, the lethal chanciness of battle did not lead to hopelessness. The survival instinct kicked in. Horrendous wounds could immobilize a man, leaving him writhing in agony. But combatants knew that quick medical care was often the difference between life and death, and so they dragged themselves to the rear. They refused to stay down and die. Studies showed that it might only take a few minutes before a sailor succumbed to hypothermia in the freezing Atlantic, but interviews with survivors later revealed that married men lasted longer than single men in the water. It was surmised that the married men had something extra to live for, and refused to go under.

Being captured by the enemy was one of the most challenging of war's experiences. The tide of battle sweeps back and forth, with soldiers overrun in extended positions or counterattacking forces. Airmen could expect almost certain capture when their planes were shot down over Europe.

Becoming a prisoner was fraught with danger. There were infamous stories of Canadian airmen parachuting to safety only to be executed by enraged German civilians bent on revenge for their now burned cities. There were shocking documented acts of Japanese soldiers killing helpless wounded soldiers and nurses after the fall of Hong Kong, and 156 confirmed cases of captured Canadian infantrymen executed after the battle during the opening days of the Normandy campaign. Even to survive the grey zone of moving from combatant to prisoner—and being accepted by the enemy as such instead of being executed on the battlefield—was fraught with danger. The act of becoming a prisoner was emasculating and dehumanizing.

For the nearly eight thousand Canadian prisoners of war, conditions in the camps were always terrible, with a constant struggle for adequate food and clothing, and ongoing battles against boredom and brutality. For already

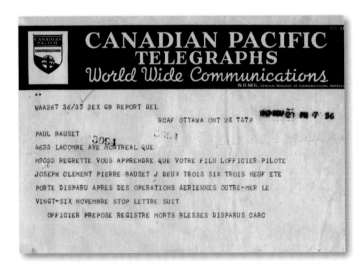

weakened men, the threat of disease always loomed, and with little medical care or drugs, minor illnesses could lead to death. The Japanese were particularly brutal toward Canadians, and many prisoners were worked to death as they suffered from malnutrition, disease, and the cruelty of vindictive guards. Red Cross packages helped to keep many prisoners alive, but all fought private wars to sustain themselves. Prisoners crafted items of hope, smuggled in parts to create radios to listen to the war, and planned escapes. In the worst camps, they choked back uncooked food and bugs to keep from starving to death.

Those who survived the battlefield or incarceration had new battles to fight upon returning home. The war had imprinted itself on their bodies. Many veterans suffered long-term effects to their health from the physical strain of war; others were forced to deal with a slow recovery from wounds. Young men appeared old and worn beyond their years; their eyes betrayed what they had seen and done. Most veterans had some form of mental trauma.

No one could escape the war. Some veterans stayed silent about their experiences for decades. Yet still the war came back to haunt at night, in dreams, and sometimes during the day. The backfire of a car or the shriek of machinery might send a veteran into a private war of the mind. Innocuous sights and smells triggered memories of service. It was not always bad—there was much pleasure to be had in reliving the camaraderie and fond memories of service to country—but there was one certainty: survival did not allow for forgetting.

Telegram, dated November 27, 1943, reporting the disappearance of Pierre Bauset in aerial action.

Al Wallace

BORN » TORONTO, ONTARIO

BRANCH » NO. 419 (MOOSE) SQUADRON,
ROYAL CANADIAN AIR FORCE

TRADE » MID-UPPER GUNNER

HOMETOWN » RICHMOND HILL, ONTARIO

Al Wallace and his crew from No. 419 (Moose) Squadron were shot down and captured by the Germans in 1943. Transferred to the infamous *Stalag Luft III* prisoner of war camp, Wallace assisted in the Great Escape.

After we were shot down they took me out into an office to be interrogated by a [German] officer. He knew more about the war than I did, and more about our bombing squadron. He knew who our commanding officer was and how many aircraft we could put up on a maximum effort. He knew far more about the air base than I did.

I was only there a few days. I was taken out, put into a compound with other prisoners and then, a few days later, we went on a train trip. I ended up at *Stalag Luft III* [a *Luftwaffe* POW camp near Zagan, Poland], where the Great Escape took place. It was just a great barbed-wire enclosure, at least fifteen acres. It was a brand-new camp. It had only opened in April 1943 and I was arriving in May. It had about 700 or 800 men in it when I arrived, but it would eventually have about 1,800 or 1,900.

It was a big camp, with double barbed-wire fences around it—two fences about ten feet apart. In between the two fences were great coils of barbed wire, literally impossible to get through. There were guard towers at different points all around the camp. They had machine guns in the towers and searchlights, which were on all night.

I made arrangements with the guy that was in charge of the block that I was in to move to another room. I moved to block 104. The room I moved to was the room where the tunnel started. I didn't know it at the time, of course, because I was quite a newcomer, and everything about the escape was secretive. Even some of the chaps in the room had nothing to do with the tunnel.

There was one chap named Pat Langford in that particular room. He was called the Tunnel *Führer*. When they were going to open the tunnel to send men down or bring men out or take sand out, he was the one that opened and

Air-Gunner class at No. 1 Bombing and Gunnery School, Jarvis, Ontario, June 1943. Wallace is in back row, third from the right.

"Fifty of the seventy-six were just murdered. They were taken out in small groups and just shot in the back of the head."

closed the tunnel. It wasn't a very good room to live in because when the tunnel was opened, there were blankets all over the floor to catch any sand and the room was in effect off limits—you couldn't go back and forth into it. I was in that room for two to three months and then I made arrangements to move out of there.

I did do a little bit of work on the tunnel. A few times I had the bags of sand down my pant legs and was disposing of it out in our garden or on the circuit that we walked around the perimeter of the camp.

Everybody in the camp knew what was going to happen on the day they were going to break out. Throughout the day, everybody in hut 104 moved out, except the men that were going to be going out. All of the men that had been selected to go moved into that hut through the day. That night, when they opened the tunnel to the surface, they had some delays. They had a hard time breaking through to the surface and then, when the tunnel opened, they found out that they were short. They thought they

were going to be within the pine trees around the camp, but they were about twenty feet short. Fortunately, they were about thirty feet behind one of the guardhouses. There was a guard in it, of course, with a searchlight, but he was shining it into the camp, so he really wasn't a problem.

But the Germans also had guards on foot outside the main wire around the camp. They walked around with their guns, back and forth. So they arranged timing and a rope: one of the men went out the tunnel and into the woods, and when the guards had turned and were walking away, he would pull the cord. One or two men in the tunnel would jump out and into the woods. They were able to get seventy-six out that way.

Through the night, an air raid took place on Berlin. Whenever there was an air raid, all the lights went out. So the lights in the tunnel went out and things were stopped for an hour or so. And then they had a couple of cave-ins when people going through knocked the supporting

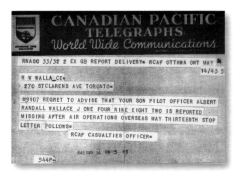

boards in the tunnel. So they had to be repaired. So these little hang-ups slowed things down.

I remember that night. I don't think I slept much because I knew the tunnel break was taking place and I just wondered when things were going to happen. Well, sure enough, around five in the morning, I heard a rifle shot, one single shot. And I said, "Oh, that's probably it." Well, that was it. One of the guards on duty around the camp veered off toward the tunnel—he was going to have a leak, you see—and he nearly fell in the hole, he was so close to it. And just at that moment, the boys got their signals mixed up. The one in the woods had pulled the cord and the one inside thought that was the clearance to pop out. He jumped out of the tunnel right in front of this guard, and the guard—I guess he must have been quite shocked—whipped his rifle up and fired a shot. He missed the man, but from there, the tunnel was over.

Fifty of the seventy-six were just murdered. They were taken out in small groups and shot in the back of the head. That was how they went. The Germans didn't admit that; they just said that they were shot while trying to escape. When our commanding officer was told, he said, "Well, how many were wounded?" "None," the Germans said, "they were all killed." That told us right away that they had been murdered. The camp all knew immediately and we wore black bands for several weeks afterwards to signify to the Germans that we knew what had happened.

It was a tough time around the camp because so many people had lost friends. A lot of them had been prisoners for three or four years, and all of sudden, their lives were blotted out, boom, like that. It was a tough time in the camp.

David Havard

BORN » VICTORIA, BRITISH COLUMBIA

BRANCH » 5TH FIELD REGIMENT,
ROYAL CANADIAN ARTILLERY, CANADIAN ARMY

TRADE » FORWARD OBSERVATION SIGNALLER

HOMETOWN » SMITHERS, BRITISH COLUMBIA

David Havard witnessed the destruction of the city of Caen and participated in the brutal fighting to liberate the Scheldt Estuary, but his most vivid memories are of the suffering of the Dutch people, mercilessly starved by their German occupiers.

We landed near Caen, which was just a shambles from being shelled by our shells and their shells and their bombs and our bombs. It was just this mass of rubble, quite an eye opener.

When you're young and immature, you think you're invincible, as I did. We were lined up in convoy and moving along beside our infantry and one of the fellows that I had been in training with was just across from me. I was talking to him and all of a sudden, a shell dropped and a piece of shrapnel killed him instantly. And I suddenly become aware that I was no longer invincible. And that's the rude awakening you get when you're young, in the service.

I was in the field artillery and the field artillery supports an infantry regiment. We supported the Black Watch [the Royal Highland Regiment of Canada]. When they needed artillery fire to help them, that's what our guns did. I was with an officer called the forward observation officer who goes up to the front and looks for places where they could see what was going on and then tells the guns where to fire the shells. I was the radio operator who sent the fire orders down to the guns. That was my job.

We travelled in a thing called a Bren gun carrier, which was a light tracked vehicle with quarter-inch armoured plate around it but the top was all open. We travelled all through Europe in this thing. There were four of us: a driver, the officer, an assistant who double-checked his calculations, and I was the signaller who sent down the fire orders when an officer decided where he wanted the shells to go. We virtually lived in that Bren gun carrier. Sometimes I went as long as forty-eight hours without any sleep because the radio had to be on twenty-four hours a day. A lot of time, I just slept sitting up.

Havard (middle) and comrades, holding hook rug in Rottingdean,
England, circa 1943–44.

It was quite a dangerous job. We had a whip aerial, like a fishing rod that sat up above the carrier by the radio. It had to be replaced a number of times because flying shrapnel would cut it off. The Germans had Hitler Youth. They were suicidal almost. After we cleared a town, some of them would stay behind as snipers in buildings and shoot at you as we were going through. And I was sniped at two or three times, but they missed me. So I was lucky.

We went into Belgium after France. We went through part of Normandy. And then into Belgium, near Antwerp, around that area in the Scheldt Estuary. It was pretty hectic there, a lot of shelling from the enemy. And they had, by that time, started sending over what we called "buzz bombs." They were unmanned bombs that flew through the air and all of a sudden dove onto their target. And then a little later, they started shelling, sending over what we call V2s. The buzz bombs were called V1s. And the V2s made no noise at all, they just came out of the sky and crashed all over the place. You got no warning at all.

"And I suddenly became aware that I was no longer invincible. And that's the rude awakening you get when you're young, in the service."

When we first went into Antwerp, it had been freed by the British. But the Scheldt Estuary, the mouth of Antwerp, was still occupied by the Germans and that's who we had to get out. And once the Germans had gone, they started shelling Antwerp with these V2s, and it became like a ghost town. Everybody went into their basements or cellars or wherever they could get and it was just a real sombre place.

All their food had gone. Many in the big cities like Amsterdam actually starved to death. A lot of people starved to death. And they were freezing too because all the coal had been taken. There was a Jewish section in Amsterdam and the Jews had been taken away and their homes had been left. The people in Holland were freezing to death and they started tearing down these buildings and using the wood to make fires to heat their places with. That's how serious it was.

We had a Mardi Gras at one place, a sort of a celebrating situation, and we had free hamburgers. And the Dutch were so hungry. We gave them food, but they were so hungry that they were just like birds. We were well fed and they'd pick up anything we dropped on the ground. They were just like birds looking for food.

The awful thing about war is I really think the civilians take the worst beating. They had to leave their homes and their homes got ransacked. And I don't know what happened to those people after the war, how they got it started up again, if they survived. And I don't know where they went, to tell you the truth, but they left their homes vacant and you'd go into a home and there would be kids' toys on the floor where they'd been left when they'd been rushed out and taken away to someplace safer. That's what it was like in Holland.

Opposite (top): Rest break in a shelter, prior to crossing the Rhine River. Left to right: Havard, Captain Billo, Gunner Mikolash, and Gunner Humphries (kneeling).

Opposite (bottom left): Letter from Major General E.G. Weeks to Havard's mother, October 29, 1946.

Opposite (bottom right): Havard in Victoria, British Columbia, May 1942.

Joe Friedman

BORN » MONTREAL, QUEBEC
BRANCH » NO. 195 SQUADRON, ROYAL AIR FORCE
TRADE » TAIL GUNNER
HOMETOWN » BAIE-D'URFÉ, QUEBEC

Hailing from a large Jewish family, Joseph Friedman enlisted in the air force at the tender age of seventeen. On December 12, 1944, on just his fourth operational flight, the Germans shot down his Lancaster near Witten. After nearly bailing out "without a parachute," the tail gunner, the only survivor from his crew of seven, became a prisoner of war.

I was born July 5, 1925, in Montreal. I came from a big family. We were nine kids, but the three older children went into the services. One brother was an airplane radio mechanic. He was in the air force. Another one was an air-frame mechanic and my sister was a wireless operator. She was stationed in Prince Edward Island during part of the war. I was at home. I was a rebellious kid, unhappy. I thought the war would be an adventure. Who knows, I might have ended up a hero. So I signed up.

I signed my parents' signature. I was underage. When they found out, they wanted to expose me and I threatened that I would join the merchant marine because the merchant marine was taking them at seventeen, no questions asked. So they relented and I continued on.

I was attached to the Royal Air Force [RAF]. Part of the crew were Canadian, part were British. The station we flew out of was Wratting Common. That's in Cambridgeshire, about seventeen kilometres from Cambridge.

I was shot down on my fourth flight. Witten was the target, and it was a town of fifty thousand people. We're now in December 1944. I remember vividly the briefing we had. We were told it was a town that had escaped any effects of the war; that the purpose of going there was to bomb it because they manufactured small arms; that would be pistols, rifles, machine guns.

We were four hundred planes that went out and bombed a town of fifty thousand. At that time, we thought that was our duty and we did it and there was no question about it. In retrospect, it was a pretty heavy-handed attack on a very miniscule target, but that's the way the war was

fought. Both sides were doing cruel things. There's nothing sweet or easy about war, and there's nobody fighting clean wars anymore.

We were attacked by Focke-Wulf 190s. That's one of the best planes that the Germans had—fighter planes. I was a tail gunner, so you have to straighten the turret out and crawl back and get your parachute and clip it on. As I was going through the tail section, crawling back to get it, I was wounded. Apparently, when the plane was hit, my parachute must have fallen off the hook or the seating, but I hadn't seen that and I ran to the door to go and get out. I didn't have my parachute when I was doing this—I must have been in a kind of shock. I couldn't open the door to squeeze through. But had the door opened, I would have jumped.

Above: Friedman's prison-camp registration card, issued at *Stalag Luft I*, Barth, Pomerania, Germany, mid-January 1945.

Left: This photograph appeared in a 1943 issue of the *Montreal Star* accompanied by the caption "Fighting Friedmans." Left to right: Melvin, Ruth, Jack, and Joe Friedman.

> *"There's nothing sweet or easy about war, and there's nobody fighting clean wars anymore."*

There was flames and I was scared and I, I didn't know. But it got stuck. Apparently, there's a kind of sheet on the bottom of the Lancaster, and as I opened the door, it kind of corrugated. And the door wouldn't open. At that moment, I realized what I was doing: I'm jumping without a parachute. I turned around and I look on the floor of the plane and there was the parachute. I hooked it on, stepped down on the corrugated metal, opened the door, and jumped.

It was a daylight raid and they saw me coming down. I landed at the end of what might have been a cultivated field. They were waiting for me. There were civilians and a couple of what I think were *Wehrmacht* [German armed forces personnel]. The soldiers got to me a step or two ahead of the civilians. The civilians were very angry. You have to remember, we were bombing their homes, their women and children. It wasn't a happy time for them and they were very angry at airmen.

They shipped me to *Dulag Luft*, an interrogation centre. They put me on a train and we went diagonally across Germany to the Baltic coast. It was a prison camp with over ten thousand prisoners of war. Maybe more than that. There were four compounds in it. Three compounds were American and one compound was the Commonwealth forces.

It was an officers' camp. I was lucky, as a sergeant, because I think as bad as things were—and things were pretty bleak, you know—we were better off than those who were not in an officers' camp. I was there until the end of the war, until I was flown out. If I had been picked up by the *Gestapo* (secret police), I would never have seen the light of day.

Opposite: Friedman's crew posing near their Wellington Bomber. Top row: Bob White (wireless operator); Norm Waring (bomb aimer); Taite Roth (pilot); George Barry (navigator). Bottom row: Friedman (tail gunner), Mark Goldwater (mid-upper gunner). Except for Friedman, all of these men were killed in action on December 12, 1944.

Armand Émond

BORN » MONTREAL, QUEBEC
BRANCH » LES FUSILIERS MONT-ROYAL, CANADIAN ARMY
TRADE » INFANTRYMAN
HOMETOWN » MONTREAL, QUEBEC

The Second Canadian Infantry Division's August 19, 1942, attack on the French port of Dieppe resulted in the virtual destruction of Armand Émond's regiment, Les Fusiliers Mont-Royal. The few who survived were taken prisoner and held for nearly three years.

For the Dieppe Raid, our job was to blow up the casino. We had Bangalore torpedoes—that's what they called them. It was TNT.

The minute they opened the boat door, we were hit with artillery. Sixteen men stayed in the boat, in the LCT (landing craft tank), so only six or seven remained. The rest were all dead. When we went ashore, we couldn't see the Germans. They were all well hid in cement bunkers. So we were a good target for them.

I disembarked at 5:40 in the morning and by 2:40 in the afternoon, we were taken as prisoners. It was Brigadier Southam who raised the white flag; we were about to drown since the tide was coming in. We started with three hundred sailors, but afterwards only about fifty or so remained.

We spent thirty-two months in Poland and fourteen months in handcuffs! We worked from eight in the morning until six at night. We worked in the woods. Then, in the summer during the harvest, we would start working at six in the morning and work until six at night, since the German guard, he told us, "Any prisoners who refuse to work will be shot!" So we worked twelve hours per day and then the autumn grain and potato harvest began, and we began working a bit later. We worked six days a week. Between us, as prisoners, the relationships were very solid. We were like brothers.

Before being liberated, we walked from Poland all the way to Germany during seven weeks. Sometimes we would get to eat a little something, since we would see a field of carrots or something and we would go dig up the carrots and eat them. They called it the "death march." Some people died along the way. The Germans didn't want

the prisoners to be taken by the Russians, so they took us to Germany. Meanwhile, the Russians were approaching on the other side. Even the Germans—the soldiers—didn't want to be captured by the Russians, so they went to the Americans' side. It was General Patton's army who encircled us. We were surrounded by the American Army. That's what saved us! When we arrived face to face with the American tanks, they saw that we were Canadian and British because of the khakis we were wearing, so they let us through. The German guards who were with us threw down their rifles and shouted in German, *"der krieg ist fertig,"* which means, "the war is over."

The greatest day of my life was April 13: liberation day. For me, that was the best birthday present. Three days before, I was with René Cardinal and since I knew we were in Germany, I said to him, "For my birthday, I hope that the war will be over!" That made him laugh. I remember that I wasn't wrong. Oh my goodness, what a relief! I didn't want to be at war anymore.

Top right: Émond and fellow prisoners of war, planting potatoes in Poland, 1944.
Top left: Émond, left, cutting wood with fellow prisoners of war, Poland, 1944.
Émond and his granddaughter, Emye Lie Émond Ubé, at Dieppe, France, in August 2009.

Bob Johnson

BORN » WINNIPEG, MANITOBA
BRANCH » NO. 28 SQUADRON, ROYAL AIR FORCE
TRADE » PILOT
HOMETOWN » CHARLOTTETOWN, PRINCE EDWARD ISLAND

Air force–pilot Robert Johnson served in India and Burma. The defining experience of his war was being shot down on a sortie over the Irrawaddy River in 1944. After parachuting, he evaded the Japanese for twenty-three nights in the jungle, eventually making his way to the Allied lines.

I was in the Canadian Army for a little better than a year, after which I obtained a discharge [so I could] re-enlist in the air force, which I did on about New Year's Eve of 1940. I was posted overseas. Things weren't so brisk. The Battle of Britain was just over and there wasn't that great a need for pilots. They'd had time to do all the fill-ins, so I wasn't immediately posted. But about four weeks later, they asked if there were any single-engine pilots who would like to volunteer for service overseas.

Seventeen of us filled the order and we were all posted. We weren't told where we were going, but within a day or so of being at sea, we learned that we were going to the Far East. Myself and another chap were posted to 28 RAF Squadron and were serving with the RAF [Royal Air Force] without much contact at all with the Canadian branch of the air force. We went immediately into operations and I wound up in the Imphal Valley [in the state of Manipur, India].

We were strictly on [Hawker] Hurricanes. That's a single-seater fighter. We were mostly armed with four twenty-millimetre cannons. Our duties varied with the demand, and we did a lot of just strict reconnaissance—searching out the Japanese, determining their movements and shooting them up as we saw fit. Other times, we'd do aerial photography.

Generally, we operated in pairs, two aircraft. The lead aircraft would do the actual reconnaissance, and the second one would watch the sky for an aerial attack. Their fighters were single-engine fighters. They were very good—a little faster than we were, and a little more manoeuvrable in some aspects. Flying in a formation of two, you didn't hang around or have to tangle with half a

Johnson and his wife Shirley, Charlottetown, 2010.

dozen or more. You had to fight your way out of whatever action you got into and then get home. Our losses were reasonably heavy. It wasn't every day that someone was getting shot down, but very often. If they didn't get back you never saw them again. They just disappeared into the jungle. cut 1 line

I was on a long-range sortie—I was a flight commander by that time—and I was about to break in a new pilot to our squadron. He was quite an experienced pilot, but had not been on operational flights. I guess I was about 150 miles away from my base, investigating roads for the movement of Japanese and whatever else we could find. I found a good-sized river craft on the Irrawaddy River [in Burma]. We were low flying down the Irrawaddy, about twenty-five feet off the water and up a little stream. I had a quick look at a ship being loaded with some stuff, but I didn't have time to call my number two. I wheeled in there and was taking a quick snap of this boat being loaded with petrol and oil drums—we had cameras mounted on our aircraft. I was doing a steep turn around the mast of this

Somewhere in "Boima"   (Can) J.7810 F/Lt. Johnson R.G.
No.28 Sqdn. R.A.F. S.E.A.C.

Feb 3/45

Dear Shirl:-

Must apologize once more for long lapse of letters but darling you can't imagine how lucky I am to be here writing this. For a month odd I was one of those nondescript characters one often reads about in bottom corners of the front page, "One of our pilots failed to return." I felt ever so sorry for my folks who would immediately receive a "missing cable and then worry until the next one arrived. But for all well C'est la Guerre." Naturally can't tell you events or circumstances concerning recent experience but might say "It was a long hard ... I won." Ended up finally slightly ... looking like a poplar tree in ... ight 130 lbs. Not much meat on a frame ... funny part was the fine beard I ... ave it on till I get to Cal. then go to ... esser & say "The works kid." Leaving ... orrow for a Medical Board & sick leave. ... ad to break off and dash away. Here I ... uite sick at tummy for a few days but ... l much better and am so happy to be ... carcely contain myself. In fact I felt ... st do some good deed ... in thankfulness so

Lieut. Shirl S. Stevens
...
Montreal
...
Montreal

Betty Drummond
4129 Dorchester W.
Apt. 9

Sender's
Name: R.G. Johnson
Rank: Flt.
No.: J.7810
Written in: ENGLISH (Language)

THESE CARDS ARE FOR THE USE OF H.M. FORCES ONLY

Single-Engine Aircraft				Multi-Engine Aircraft							Pass-enger	Inst./Cloud Flying (Incl. in cols. (1) to (10))	
DAY		NIGHT		DAY			NIGHT						
DUAL	PILOT	DUAL	PILOT	DUAL	1st PILOT	2nd PILOT	DUAL	1st PILOT	2nd PILOT			DUAL	PILOT
(1)	(2)	(3)	(4)	(5)	(6)	(7)	(8)	(9)	(10)	(11)		(12)	(13)

COMMENDATORY ENDORSEMENT.

CAN. J.7810. F/LT. R.G. JOHNSON - 28 SQUADRON.

"On 18th April 1944 whilst on an Offensive Reconnaissance sortie in the KOHIMA area F/Lt.Johnson went to attack a ground target. On firing, the starboard cannon exploded causing extensive damage to the wing. The pilot found that he was unable to gain height and that the stalling speed on the starboard wing was 165 m.p.h. Having at first decided to bale out he reconsidered his decision and by skilful use of controls managed to bring the aircraft to an aerodrome where he effected a successful wheels up landing at a speed of 170 m.p.h. F/Lt.Johnson's decision and skill in saving the aircraft is worthy of the highest praise".

Air Commodore,
Air Officer Commanding,
NO.221 GROUP, ROYAL AIR FORCE.

Dated:- 1st June 1944.

"There was a boom-boom and a hole between my feet and up behind the instrument panel and I was suddenly aware that I was losing altitude."

thing, snapping my camera, when I was hit with anti-aircraft fire. There was a *boom-boom* and a hole between my feet and up behind the instrument panel and I was suddenly aware that I was losing altitude. I was going to have to come down.

By that time we were maybe two hundred miles from our base. I managed to gain a little altitude before I started to overheat. I had got just across the Irrawaddy and was able to contact my number two by radio. I told him I was being forced to bail out. I had been hit, and by that time I was burning, so I was leaving the aircraft. He said, "Good luck, old chap." That's the last I heard of him.

I did bail out. I was at low level, quite low, and I managed a safe landing. I ditched my parachute and grabbed my escape kit and started running. Immediately, I was being chased, but I had about a five-hundred-foot head start. I hid in some low bush in a crevice in the ground. I dove in there and just lay still. They came all around me, but they didn't find me. That was about nine in the morning.

I was there until a couple of hours after dark, and then I got out.

I decided eventually that I was going to walk at night and not in the daytime. I had good maps with me, so I walked for the next twenty-three nights. I got away with it. I was sent back to my unit, but within a few days, I was ordered to undertake a trip around all the local squadrons in that part of Burma, to tell my story of how to survive in the jungle.

Opposite: Letter from Johnson to his wife, Shirley, on February 8, 1945; Compass used by Johnson in Burma; Commendation awarded to Johnson, June 1, 1944.

Lou Howard

BORN » SELKIRK, MANITOBA

BRANCH » HMCS SARNIA, ROYAL CANADIAN NAVY

TRADE » NAVIGATION/ASDIC OFFICER

HOMETOWN » OTTAWA, ONTARIO

Less than one month before the end of the war against Germany, on April 16, 1945, the Nazi U-boat *U-190* sank the Canadian minesweeper HMCS *Esquimalt* in the approaches to Halifax harbour. Of the seventy-one man crew, forty-four perished in part due to the fact that it took hours for *Esquimalt*'s sister ship, HMCS *Sarnia*, to learn that she had been lost. Lou Howard was the navigation and ASDIC, or sonar, officer onboard the *Sarnia* that day.

I went active in the navy in December 1942. I went in as an ordinary seaman and somehow, during the training process, I was spotted and asked to sit for an officers' board and I must have aced the board because before I knew it, I was taken out of a hammock and I was outfitted in probationary officer's accommodation. I was sent on officer training at King's College and *Cornwallis* [Nova Scotia] and other places.

I got out of the lower deck and went up to become the navigating officer and the ASDIC [or sonar] officer of HMCS *Sarnia*. We were on convoy duty and I had the pleasure of being frozen to death in the North Atlantic—not frozen to death, but really, really cold—shepherding ships in convoys from Halifax. We went from Halifax to south of Iceland, which was called West OMP—West Ocean Meeting Place—and then we would pick up ships coming back from England. We'd meet the mid-Atlantic escort group and transfer our ships to them, and they would transfer the empties to us. We'd take them back to either New York or Boston or Sydney or someplace or other.

We were taken off the convoy escort task force, and put on local Halifax defence force at the end of March 1945, because a submarine had been found outside the gates of Halifax by the interception of communications between the submarine and the headquarters in Germany. So dockyard said, "There's a sub out there, so you guys go out on a search and destroy mission." On April 14, 1945, the captain of the *Esquimalt* came over and we sat in the boardroom, talked about having to sail on the search and

"In those days, I could read the Morse code sent by lamps. There was a great big airplane flew over and it said, 'Survivors ahead, survivors ahead.'"

OFFICERS ON DUTY APRIL 16

HMCS *Sarnia* officers on duty, April 16, 1945. Left to right: Shonfield, Kirby, Douty, Salter, Brown, Cantril, Howard.

"Forty-four young men died that day...because somebody was not at his job in Halifax. "

destroy mission the next morning. On April 15, we both sailed at 0800. We had agreed at our meeting that *Sarnia* and *Esquimalt* would meet at a place we called "C buoy." We both knew where it was—a buoy in the water just past the gates of Halifax. We had agreed we were going to meet at 0800 on April 16.

On April 16 at 0800, *Esquimalt* was not to be found. We couldn't raise her by radio telegraphy. We told the dockyard, which was "Captain D" in those days, that *Esquimalt* had not appeared and we asked that they send out planes from Shearwater [Nova Scotia] to find out where *Esquimalt* was. We later learned that *Esquimalt* had been torpedoed at 0637 on April 16. And they'd gone down in about four minutes. The radio operator had no opportunity to send a message or distress signal.

Between that time, when we sent the message to Halifax dockyard saying we can't raise *Esquimalt*, we got a couple of ASDIC contacts and we were at action stations and dropping depth charges. By 10:30, dockyard finally

woke up and said, "Have you found *Esquimalt*?" And we said, "No, please send planes out of Shearwater." At noon that day, a plane came over. In those days, I could read the Morse code sent by lamps. There was a great big airplane flew over and it said, "Survivors ahead, survivors ahead." We picked up twenty-seven crew members who were alive and thirteen crew members who were dead. Forty-four young men died that day in thirty-four-degree water, because somebody was not at his job in Halifax on that morning.

Top left: Howard's family. Top row, left to right: Wiltrude, Claire, Newman, and Graham Gowan. Bottom row, left to right: Marj., Lou, Ewa.
Top right: Howard with (on left) RCAF Flight Lieutenant Basil Stead, HMCS *Sarnia*.
Bottom left: Two Carley floats carrying survivors from the sinking of the HMCS *Esquimalt*.
Bottom right: A survivor from HMCS *Esquimalt* going ashore from HMCS *Sarnia*, Halifax, Nova Scotia, April 16, 1945. Note some of the dead from the *Esquimalt* in the background.

167

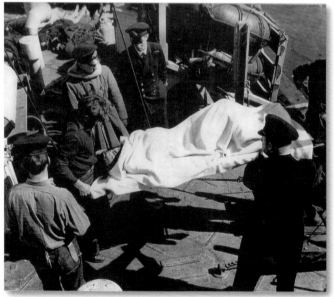

Howard Large

BORN » LEAMINGTON, ONTARIO

BRANCH » THE ESSEX SCOTTISH REGIMENT,
CANADIAN ARMY

TRADE » BREN GUNNER

HOMETOWN » KINGSVILLE, ONTARIO

Howard Large went ashore at Dieppe on August 19, 1942, with the Essex Scottish Regiment. After being wounded in the foot, he was captured by the Germans and spent nearly three years as a prisoner of war.

We went to Bognor Regis [England] and that's where we got our orders to go to Dieppe. We went aboard the ships the first time in July and then they cancelled it—bad weather. The first time, we cheered like the devil when they said we were on our way over. But the second time, there wasn't a cheer. It was just silence.

We landed in the early sunrise and they were just bombarding us. They knew we were coming because the big guns were going and the smaller guns were going and the machine guns were going and everything. The noise was something. Then we hit the beach. Some of us got in; some of us got hit right in the water.

We got in and got up to the wall. The engineers were with us and they had ten-foot-long pipes they called Bangalore torpedoes [obstacle-clearing explosives]. They threw them up on top of the barbed wire. They ignited one and it started slipping back toward us. One of our fellows, Everett McCormick from Leamington [Ontario], reached up and was pushing it back, but it kept coming. He stood there and held it, and got himself blown up. He should have had a decoration.

That was my first real blow. The shooting was going on and that, but it didn't bother me. But to get blown right up, that sort of got to me for a bit.

About twenty of us made a dash for the houses, and seven of us made it. The rest were all piled up all along the way. We went inside. A German patrol came in the building. Sergeant Leopold just said, "Wait until I say fire." The seven of us fired our guns—the Bren gun [light machine gun] and rifles—right down the hallway. They had come in and they were laughing and that. And then there was no more laughing, not even a moan. We got the whole patrol.

"About twenty of us made a dash for the houses, and seven of us made it. The rest were all piled up along the way."

That's when they finally said, "Howard, look at your foot." The blood was just squirting out of it. I had to cut my laces with my bayonet. I got my foot out and put my field dressings on it. I used my knife and scabbard and my rifle sling and put a tourniquet on my leg. I couldn't move very well, so I went down to the basement of the house. I took the rest of my grenades and I buried them in the [dirt] floor and waited. Then, all of a sudden, I heard a patrol coming. I yelled that I was wounded and all I got was gunshots coming down. When they quit firing, I yelled again, and they fired again. They fired down there about three times. Then they came down and got me out.

It was another German patrol. When I got upstairs and they went to take me out, the dead bodies of the other fellows were there. One soldier put the rifle right to my head and I thought, this is it. Another soldier just reached up and grabbed a hold of the rifle and he said, in English, "This is my prisoner." He made the other fellow help me over the bodies, because I couldn't walk very well and

I'd lost my tourniquet. They took me down to where they were taking the wounded out in front of the building and put me on the lawn. On the way, a lady came out of the house with a tray of beer and offered it to us. They handed me one before they took one themselves. The best beer I ever had, right until this day.

 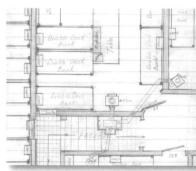

Above left: Large's second cousin, Linda. The picture arrived in the mail while Large was incarcerated as a POW at *Stalag IX*, 1943.
Above right: Large, 2009.
Bottom: Sketch of the POW camp by E.B. "Ted" Walsh. Floor plan of one wing in the POW camp.

Malcolm MacConnell

BORN » PLASTER ROCK, NEW BRUNSWICK

BRANCH » NO. 50 SQUADRON; NO. 97 (PATHFINDER) SQUADRON, ROYAL AIR FORCE

TRADE » PILOT

HOMETOWN » DARTMOUTH, NOVA SCOTIA

Born into a military family, Malcolm MacConnell joined the air force in 1942 and trained as a pilot. His first Bomber Command operation, with No. 50 Squadron of the Royal Air Force, came just days after the invasion of Normandy. Over his next thirty-eight operational flights in 1944 and 1945, MacConnell survived close calls and lost many comrades, as well as his younger brother.

I was posted to England in 1943 and on June 14th, 1944, eight days after D-Day, I was assigned to 50 Royal Air Force Squadron and I flew with that squadron for two and a half months, at which time I had put in twenty-one operations on Bomber Command on Lancasters, on both French and German targets. The last day of August, I was transferred to 97 Pathfinder Squadron, where I flew another seventeen operations before the end of the war.

Sometimes, we were bombing a city. Often, we were bombing the VI buzz bomb sites, their storage areas and the launching pads. We would bomb their oil refineries and oil plants. We would bomb railway yards, communication systems, specific factories in an area. On a few occasions, two occasions specifically, we bombed shipping.

We never broke radio silence, ever. We were briefed, and we went out by ourselves. The majority of our flights were by night, and you were alone. Occasionally, another aircraft would come close enough so that you could see it was a friendly aircraft, but mostly you were alone until you got into the target area. Then, with searchlights, flares that were being dropped to identify the target, flak bursts, and so on, you would see many more aircraft. You'd realize more people were around you, a lot more aircraft. Once the bombing was over and you got away from the target area, you seemed to be alone again, in the darkness.

I had a very good crew, but with the flak and fighters around, I felt fear—deep fear, terror. But after a little experience, I found that I was able to cope—recognize the fear, recognize everything happening in my surroundings and sort of cope and react and do things.

"[A]fter a little experience, I found that I was able to cope—recognize the fear, recognize everything happening in my surroundings and sort of cope ..."

Once out of the danger, that fear subsided almost instantly. And yes, I knew that I was bombing people, but I did not ever dwell on the fact that people were being killed. I was thinking of the damage that I was doing to the enemy's war effort.

One day we went to bomb a target in daylight and this big cloud was moving easterly. It was believed that by the time we got to the target area, the cloud would be gone. But we got there and the target was still solidly covered by clouds. Our controller told us to keep on course. We flew for about twenty minutes or more and then he gave us an order: a very shallow turn to starboard through 180 degrees to fly back over the area of the target.

I didn't like flying in that because we were in a very close formation. And I kept descending very slowly, going down and down and down, and finally I thought, well, I'll

MacConnell and his crew as they commenced their tour of operations with Bomber Command, June 1944. Front left to right: Norm Hawkings, Gunnar Erickson, Jimmy Aitken. Rear: MacConnell (Mac), Eddie Steel, Gil Cook, Laurie Williams.

"War is the most miserable, inhumane interaction between people."

go down just below the cloud and maybe that's a railway yard that we were supposed to be bombing. Sure enough, I come out of the clouds and just as I come out, my rear gunner says, "You know, we're supposed to bomb a railway yard, there's one right behind us, skipper." So I turned around and there it was. As I was looking to the south, heading toward the target, my eye lit on a little building about twenty by twenty and three stories high. The second my eyes hit that, something just told me, get moving, move. I pulled up hard and was climbing—turned to port to get up into the clouds, but I was too late. I was hit by the shells bursting, first one, then another, and the third or fourth one hit me under the wing. I thought we were really done for. I was able to get back up into the clouds and I abandoned my attack. That was a very, very close one.

I came back from a raid once and picked up my mail. There was a telegram in it. My sister had graduated from nursing in April and had applied for the army nursing corps, so I said, I bet that's telling me that she had

been accepted. I pulled open the telegram. It was from my mother, saying that my brother, Bud Erlin, had been killed on the twenty-third day of July [1944]. I'd had many friends who were killed. After a while, it kind of got to be, you know, they're gone, it's too bad. Like, they broke their toe, well, that's too bad. But certainly when my brother was killed, that was deep, deep, deep, deep grief.

It's my mature conclusion that war is the most miserable, inhumane interaction between people. When I entered the air force, my primary reason was because it would be exciting, I was sure. My thinking wasn't so much that it was a deeply patriotic thing to do, but that it was sort of an exciting thing to do. But it was a very patriotic thing to do and that war was a war that had to be fought. There's some that I don't think need to be fought, but that one had to be.

MacConnell and his crewmates at war's end, May 10, 1945. Left to right: Jimmy Carter; Malcolm MacConnell; Norn Hawkings; Gunnar Erickson; Doreen Cook (wife of Gil Cook); Gil Cook; Eddie Steel; Norm Cholerton; Jimmy Aitken.

Murray T. Copot

BORN » FRASERWOOD, MANITOBA

BRANCH » HMCS ALBERNI; HMCS ONTARIO,
ROYAL CANADIAN NAVY

TRADE » LEADING CODER

HOMETOWN » CALGARY, ALBERTA

Hailing from the tiny and landlocked Ukrainian-Canadian community of Fraserwood, Manitoba, Murray T. Copot went on active service with the navy in 1942. His first vessel was the flower-class corvette, HMCS *Alberni.* Copot survived the sinking of the *Alberni,* torpedoed by *U-480* on August 21, 1944, but fifty-nine of his eighty-five crewmates were not as fortunate.

I joined up at HMCS *Chippewa* in Winnipeg. After serving some time at *Chippewa*—doing some guard duty and learning how to be a naval person, because Winnipeg is in the middle of the country and there's no ocean—I went to HMCS *York* in Toronto. After Toronto, I went to Ste.-Hyacinthe, Quebec, for my course. I was in Ste.-Hyacinthe for a few months and then I went to Halifax and the next thing I know, I'm heading down to the HMCS corvette *Alberni.* I got onto the *Alberni* and that night, we took off with a small convoy to Cape Breton. It was kind of rough and I got seasick, but that was the only time.

From then on, we were on the Triangle Run. That was between St. John's, Newfoundland, Halifax, Boston, and New York. We took convoys to a certain point in the Atlantic Ocean and then we picked up other convoys coming back. We went overseas in March 1944, and took some convoys into the English Channel. And then we were preparing for D-Day. On June 4, Captain Ian Bell—a great captain and a great person—came aboard and said, "We're not going today." On June 6, we helped take over the Mulberry dock—that was the dock that the tanks and stuff used to go ashore. We got there at about 9:30.

There are three days I would like to forget: June 6, 1944, at 9:30 in the morning on Juno Beach; August 21, 1944, when the ship was torpedoed; and September 1945, when we picked up the prisoners of war from Hong Kong.

On our off-hours, we'd play bridge. Sometimes the alarm would go off, saying that we had spotted some submarines. I don't know how we did it, but we'd put our cards down, grab our boots and jackets, and get up there. After

HMCS *Ontario* crew, November 1945.

"[A]ll at once, it started to get brighter. I said, 'Well, I'm going the right way. My mother can't get a telegram because it would kill her.'

the all-clear, we went down and started to play bridge again as if nothing happened. Sometimes we had cockroach races on the mess deck table, especially on July 1. We'd make a dollar or two or lose a dollar or two on our cockroach.

When the ship [HMCS *Alberni*] was going down, I must have got hit in the head or something. I woke up and it was kind of dark underwater. I wasn't too sure whether I was going up or down. But all at once, it started to get brighter. I said, "Well, I'm going the right way. My mother can't get a telegram because it would kill her." I popped up, and when I saw the bow of the ship going down, I broke all records in the water to get away from being sucked down again.

At that time, my mother and father were in Fraserwood, Manitoba. It was quarter to twelve, Greenwich Mean Time. My mother woke up at quarter to four Winnipeg time. She woke my dad up and said, "Something's happening to our son." They got down and started praying and it was about that time that I said, "My mother can't get a telegram because it would kill her." There's something in prayers.

Joe Hickson

BORN » WHEATLEY, ONTARIO

BRANCH » NO. 420 (SNOWY OWL) SQUADRON, ROYAL CANADIAN AIR FORCE

TRADE » TAIL GUNNER

HOMETOWN » WHEATLEY, ONTARIO

One incident stands out in Joe Hickson's mind from his service with Bomber Command during the Second World War: crash landing in the North Sea and drifting in a dinghy until rescued.

When we hit the water, I was in crash position right behind the main spar of the wing, with my back up against it. There was a bomb inspection hole between my legs, and being as the bomb doors were open, the water just shot in like a fire hose. A big wave of water came over my head and then I blacked out.

When I came to, I saw the legs of one of the crew going out the back hatch, so I said, "I better get out of here." The water was up above my chest, not up to my chin yet, but above my chest. I said to myself, "I've got to move." I scrambled back there and came out the hatch and when I did, the dinghy was out—it pops out of the wing. There were eight of us in the crew that night and they were all in the dinghy, I thought. When I jumped out, it was floating off the edge of the wing and was almost finished blowing up. Somebody said, "The skipper's not here." I grabbed the side of the dinghy and put my toes in where the dinghy had come out and held on. The waves were coming over the wing and it was blowing wind, strong wind. I looked and the skipper's walking down the fuselage. The plane is floating. It didn't smash; it made a perfect landing. My toes popped out of the hole and I said, "I can't hold it." Somebody hollered, "Don't worry, we'll catch the tail."

They caught the tail, the skipper got in and then we pushed off. But the dinghy wouldn't go. In training, we'd been taught that the plane would sink within one or two minutes, so when it wouldn't go, the wireless operator found a knife. The lines were cut and we drifted free. If the plane had sunk, it would have towed us down with it.

We floated free and off into the darkness. We looked back five minutes later and the plane was still floating. We looked a little later and it was gone. We had to get the radio, which was supposed to be floating with our other

survival equipment. We pulled those ropes in, but there was nothing on the end. Those were the ropes we'd cut.

Within a few minutes, we pretty well all got seasick. There were ten-, fifteen-foot waves—huge waves—and we were bobbing around. A wee bit of daylight was starting then, and we could see, but as soon as you'd put your head up, you'd be sick, so we just quieted down and leaned over the sides. We tried bailing some of the water out of the dinghy, but that was unsuccessful. We had nothing to dip with other than our hands.

As the morning wore on, we knew air-sea rescue would be out looking for us. We did hear planes searching and we saw these planes flying low. But being a mile or two away, we knew there was no way they would see us. We wouldn't even be a dot in the ocean. I guess some of us slept or kept quiet and later in the afternoon, the sun shone, which warmed us up a bit. Late in the afternoon, the skipper says, "Well, we're in a position. We've got to do something." We got ourselves squared around and talking

a bit. "Well," we said, "we're not going to get rescued to-day." A west wind was blowing, so we all decided it would be a good idea to get the sail up and try to sail to the coast of Holland. Then we'd have to duck the Germans.

We finally got the sail out and got it up. We saw these planes flying—[Handley Page] Halifaxes [Bombers]—and we saw them turn and head back in a westerly direction. And we said, "Well, that's it for today, they're all done searching for us." So we finished getting the sail up. There was one rope missing, but we were improvising for it. Another five, ten minutes went by, and then here come those three Halifaxes, heading right straight toward us. We started waving and shouting. They were planes from our own squadron, with PT [Patrol Torpedo] markings on them, so they were guys that had got permission to look for us.

They made another run and dropped another dinghy for us. They dropped two of them, actually. One we couldn't retrieve, but the one we got had warm suits in it. Our mid-upper gunner, he was shivering from the cold and wet.

We got him transferred and put the warm suit on him and kind of quieted him down from his shivering. The planes were circling. Three [Avro] Lancasters [Bombers] came, then came a [Vickers] Warwick [Bomber], and then they left and we thought, "Oh boy." It's getting pretty near dark now. And then came a [Lockheed] Hudson [Bomber], and underneath the Hudson, they had an airborne lifeboat. He circled a couple of times, and we thought, "He's going to drop that." Then he wiggled his wings and away he went and we were all alone. Well, boy, our spirits dropped. We thought, "Uh-oh, that's it." We thought the sea was just too rough to drop that lifeboat, so he's gone.

A few minutes went by, which seemed like an eternity, and then we saw a little seaplane coming—a [Submarine] Walrus. He made one circle and went way off, and down he come into the sea. He just disappeared, and we thought, "Oh man, he's gone." The sea was so rough, we didn't think he could possibly land in it. We kept looking and looking and finally we saw each other—I guess he was on

Squadron 420, Welsborne, England - April 1944
Left to Right: Joe Hickson, Lyle Engemone, Ian McGown, Vic Mother, Al McDonald, Jim Wigley

"So you close your eyes and all of a sudden, the motor revs up a bit and kabang, you hit something."

top of a wave. He must have been a mile away when he hit the water. He was taxiing toward us and finally got there. So we all got out of the dinghy. You go into the nose of the Walrus seaplane, because it's a pusher type, the propeller's behind, so we went in there and crawled down back. The fellow ahead of me, he went clear to the tail and I'm there too and it's only about two-foot square back there on a board. The others came in behind and the skipper was the last one to get in.

By now, it's completely dark. The Walrus starts up and is chugging along toward England. He's going and you close your eyes and you dream. Well, it's dry and it's fairly warm and you're more comfortable than you've been all day. So you close your eyes and all of a sudden, the motor revs up a bit and *kabang*, you hit something. Man, what did we hit? Your mind goes crazy on you. You think, well, we hit a mine? No, it didn't explode. Maybe a log? Debris of some sort? Okay. The motor starts up again. We only go a little bit, *kabang* again—same thing happens. What

in the world are we hitting? Somebody's pulling on my foot, so I start backing out, and I pull a jerk on the fellow in front of me.

We got out at the front of the plane and here's what he was doing: revving the motor up and hitting the back of a boat. We thought it was a PT boat, but it wasn't. It was a rescue launch that stayed in the North Sea for maybe a week at a time, just for emergencies such as ours. We transferred into it, all of us. Everybody got a shot of rum and got our wet clothes off. We put on navy blue coveralls and got into a nice warm bunk with a nice white blanket. That's what I remember.

Opposite (top): Crew Photo. Hickson is first from left.
Opposite (bottom): Halifax-3 Bomber, England, 1944.
Above: January 2010.

Art Bridge

BORN » BELLEVILLE, ONTARIO

BRANCH » THE ARGYLL AND SUTHERLAND HIGHLANDERS, CANADIAN ARMY; 3RD CANADIAN INFANTRY DIVISION MOBILE BATH AND LAUNDRY UNIT

TRADE » BREN GUNNER/MOBILE BATH ATTENDANT

HOMETOWN » QUALICUM BEACH, BRITISH COLUMBIA

Private Art Bridge of the Argyll and Sutherland Highlanders endured continuous hard fighting from Point 195 in Normandy through to the Leopold Canal: on October 14, 1944, at Watervliet, Belgium, he was stunned by German shelling. After evacuation from the line, doctors pronounced him unfit for further combat duty. He had become, in the official army parlance of the time, a neuropsychiatric casualty.

I spent my wartime career with the Argyll and Sutherland Highlanders, who went to France in July of 1944, and I discovered the reality of war, much to my horror and shock and disbelief. I was number two on the Bren gun. My buddy, he was number one. He carried the Bren gun or we shared carrying it. I had a rifle. We got through the Normandy campaign. We went up and had the battle on the Seine River, crossing near Elbeuf, and we went on up to Belgium, near Bruges and that got nasty, real nasty, at a place called Moerbrugge.

It wasn't until October 14 that we got mobile and moving, and we were ordered to cross the Leopold Canal at the eastern end. And we did that without any trouble. We got across on a broken bridge while on foot. We crossed and advanced up the road to a little town called Watervliet.

During the night, the Germans attacked us. They were firing flares and we couldn't really see them. It was a really scary night—the shells, bullets flying all over. We were in a house out alongside the road that was reasonably secure. But the next morning, when daylight came, they started an artillery bombardment. They had some big guns from the coast that turned around. The great big shells started landing all around our house and one hit the house right across the road and just about knocked us all to pieces. The next shell hit quite close to the house. I was looking out the window and the shell blast knocked me down and knocked me out—more or less stunned me. I couldn't get up. I wasn't physically affected, but I was so terrified and

shocked that I couldn't do anything. I couldn't move. It was a horrible feeling.

The RAP [regimental aid post] doctor sent me to the hospital, to a psychiatric ward. Other injured people went there for medical care; I went for psychiatric care. It was ruled that I wasn't fit for front-line duty any further, and believe me, I was relieved at that because I don't think I could have survived any more. Shortly after that episode, our unit was moved across through Antwerp and up on the Scheldt. A number of my friends became casualties. And I thought to myself, well, good God, I could've been one of them if I hadn't been declared unfit for action. I've carried that cross for years. I guess it'll never leave me.

Above: Bridge in England, 1942 (right), and Nijmegen, The Netherlands, January 1945 (left).

Top right: Bridge and his younger brother, Alan, after returning from overseas, Belleville, Ontario, 1946.

Bottom right: German bullet from the fighting at Saint-Lambert-sur-Dives, France.

They put me into a holding camp. There were a lot of people in similar condition, I was surprised to discover. They formed us into a work company. We'd go out and dig graves or load trucks with ammunition and things like that around Antwerp. The work company that I was assigned to moved into Nijmegen, up in Holland, up in the salient [the Nijmegen Salient].

Just around Christmas 1944, I was assigned to the 3rd Division Mobile Laundry and Bath Unit. I was assigned to look after the store. They were centered in Nijmegen. You can imagine the conditions there. The town had been bombed pretty badly, buildings were knocked down, and there was constant artillery shell fire coming into the town, over on the island and the other side of the river. I served with them right until the end of the war.

Allan Smith

BORN » BEAVERTON, ONTARIO

BRANCH » NO. 419 (MOOSE) SQUADRON,
ROYAL CANADIAN AIR FORCE

TRADE » BOMB AIMER

HOMETOWN » TRENTON, ONTARIO

Allan Smith was shot down over German-occupied Europe. He received assistance from French partisans, but before the Allied forces could liberate him, he was betrayed to the Germans. Treated as a spy, he endured captivity in Paris' notorious Fresnes Prison, Buchenwald concentration camp, and *Stalag Luft III*.

We had been raiding the railyard south of Paris, and had successfully dropped our bombs and were on the way home. And on the way, of course, we were hit head on with a Junkers 88 night fighter. Our aircraft was shot up quite badly and the port inner engine was on fire. All the crew bailed out successfully, and I found myself hanging in my parachute, floating over occupied France.

I hit the ground very gently and hid my chute under some underbrush. I got rid of my sidearm, a Smith and Wesson pistol, and I took off into the unknown. I didn't have a clue where I was going. I knew I was in the neighbourhood of Chartres. During the second day, wandering around, I made contact with the French resistance. The resistance hid me in the small village of Berchères-la-Maingot. I stayed with a French family.

I spent my nights in a cupboard, along with a huge spider. After almost two weeks with the French family—their name was LeGrande—I met one of the spies who was dropped in, a radio operator, code named Janette, and I did some coding for her and also fixed up her radio. About that time, it was starting to heat up in the area and people were coming to the door and inquiring if a British officer was staying with them. So the family decided I'd better move and they made arrangements that I would go to Spain, over the Pyrenees.

I was picked up in a car, along with a Belgian traitor and his red-headed girlfriend. It was July 15, and I was on my way to Paris, supposedly to have false identity papers made. We spent the night in Paris and during the night, we begin to feel that we'd been had.

The next morning, we raced through Paris in a car. I

remember passing the Eiffel Tower and all of a sudden, we ran into a roadblock—the German field police. They pulled us right out of the vehicle. They knew we were coming and they didn't treat us too friendly. They put two guards with us and told the driver to keep on going. After a short trip, we arrived at Fresnes Prison. It was a nasty piece of business: a four-storey building, containing over 1,500 cells. It was called the Gateway to the Concentration Camps: a filthy place rampant with fleas and all kinds of bugs. Executions were carried out regularly and screams could be heard all night long, along with the rifle shots of the executions.

On August 15, the prison was evacuated, including the 168 airmen. We were put on a train that would hold forty men or eight horses. The Germans put hundreds of us in each boxcar. It was five days of living hell. We were in Buchenwald concentration camp [near Weimar, Germany]. It wasn't an extermination camp like Dachau and Auschwitz; it was a labour camp. There were a couple of factories there, and they worked the people to death. And of course, there

were a lot of executions. When we were there, there were thirty-five or so French and British spies executed, and they were executing four hundred Russians a day. They were going up in smoke. We were really getting scared.

We left Buchenwald on October 20, 1944, for *Stalag [Luft] III* [a *Luftwaffe* prisoner-of-war camp near Zagan, Poland]. It was quite dicey. We were to be executed on October 21. Thank God it didn't come off. The *Luftwaffe* got us out of there. One of the *Luftwaffe* officers visited the camp hospital. The *Luftwaffe* doctor asked how we got in there. I guess he reported it to the *Luftwaffe* in Berlin and some of the higher ups. We think maybe it was Goering who stopped the execution.

So we got out of there and arrived at *Stalag III*. That was a real Sunday school compared with Buchenwald.

Left: The LeGrande family who hid Smith after he landed in occupied France, 1944.
Centre: The telegram to Smith's father, notifying him that his son had become a prisoner of war, 1945.
Right: Smith after his arrival at *Stalag Luft III* on October 21, 1944.

Bernard Finestone

BORN » MONTREAL, QUEBEC
BRANCH » THE BRITISH COLUMBIA DRAGOONS
(9TH ARMOURED REGIMENT), CANADIAN ARMY
TRADE » ARMOURED CORPS OFFICER
HOMETOWN » MONTREAL, QUEBEC

A captain with the British Columbia Dragoons, Bernard Finestone fought the elite of the German Army through the hardest battles of the Italian campaign, including the Moro River, Ortona, Monte Cassino, and the breaking of the Hitler Line.

The late 1930s were terrible times. I'm Jewish. In my mind and in my father's mind—not my mother's, oddly enough; she was very upset when I went—we felt very simply that Hitler was threatening every Jew. He was threatening Western civilization and he had to be stopped.

In the beginning, they made every officer qualify to all the trades in the tank. There were three: the driver mechanic, who drives the thing and maintains it; the gunner, who fires the seventy-five-millimetre [gun] we eventually ended up with—when we started, they were two-pounders and the machine guns; and the wireless operator, who operated the wireless and loaded the gun. Everybody had to qualify and when they did, they got trades pay.

You have orders. You have to be at such and such a line by ten and in another river by twelve, and you have targets. You do your damndest to achieve the targets. Most of the time we did, sometimes, we couldn't. Sometimes we fought to take a river and didn't succeed and had to wait and try it again the next day. But that's how it was. You were given your orders every night and you knew what you had to accomplish that day and you did your damndest to do it.

Tanks tended not to fight at night. After dark, they withdrew us. We would go back five hundred or one thousand yards and into what we'd call the "laager." We'd make a big circle facing outwards so if the Germans broke through during the night, we could fight them off. And then all our supply people would come up. We only had ninety-three rounds in a Sherman, and you could fire ninety-three rounds in a day. If you didn't get it replenished, you couldn't fire the next day. So you had to get out and re-gas and get more ammunition, and they'd bring up food. You'd get all that done, perhaps by ten or eleven,

11th Infantry Brigade liaison officer and other Canadian troops near Monte Cassino, Italy, February 1944.

and you'd dig a slit trench under the tanks so that if the shells came in, they wouldn't get you. You'd sleep in the slit trench until four, five in the morning and get up and go again. We'd get three, four, five hours sleep.

There was no friendship between them and us. As a matter of fact, it was so bad that the Germans would fire at our Red Cross. If they captured people, they wouldn't accept their surrender, they would kill them. And we got so mad, we started to behave the exact same way. All our generals would try to stop the Canadians from doing this. We said, "To hell with this, if that's the rules of the war," and we did exactly the same to the Germans. I shot down more than thirty Germans who were trying to surrender.

That was the war they fought, and we fought the war their way. If we saw an ambulance at the front and it was in a critical place, we would put a shell in it, exactly as they did to us. They damn soon learned to be careful with Canadians. When we went into the major battles, General Alexander issued an order of the day for the Canadians:

"Eight hundred shells landed the first ten days at Cassino. So we even sandbagged the crapper."

A Sherman tank from the British Columbia Dragoons, near the Moro River, Italy, December 1943.

"Start taking prisoners. Otherwise, they'll never surrender to you. You're not doing a smart thing, change it." But Canadians were tough. If the Germans did something to us, we did it to them. I bet you'll never find that comment in any history book.

They talk about post-traumatic stress disorder. Every single soldier who went into action had post-traumatic stress disorder—including me. The first time I went into action, we blew up a couple of tanks. I was so excited. I remember hammering my hand on the turret and saying, "It works, it works." I'd been training for three years. Finally, I put it into action and it worked. The Germans were on fire and I was still there. But that was the first time.

The next morning we were to go off around seven. We got to the front lines at six and from six to seven, I sat in my turret, waiting for the signal to go. I had five men in my tank and communications with the intercom, all nervous and edgy. I was trying to tell them funny stories, to keep them preoccupied. The stories weren't all that funny, but everybody laughed hysterically. The stress and strain in that waiting period was incredible. But then comes the next stage, when one of your tanks is hit and some of your men die. These are men you've spent months and years with, and you see them lying there. One of my men—I can never forget this, his guts spilling out, just lying on the ground— he asked me to hold his hand, which I did while he died. You don't recover from that. You never recover from that.

"There isn't anybody who was in real battle who came out unmarked. It took seven years before I stopped having nightmares."

Anybody who says they do is lying. They weren't there.

In my day, we didn't disqualify people because of post-traumatic stress disorder. If they couldn't fight anymore, we took them out of the tanks and sent them back to the supply line where they could do the jobs that we required. We helped them over their bad time. If they couldn't work at all, and some couldn't, they went to the psychologist. We never saw them again.

There isn't anybody who was in real battle who came out unmarked. It took seven years before I stopped having nightmares. I got married six years after and my wife used to wake me up and say, "You're screaming."

But it goes. It burns off, it disappears. Is it a pleasant thing? No. Winning is great, but the stress is murder. We've got a great number of things to be extremely proud of, but the dirty part of war is a part of war. And not to tell the truth, not to carry the stories out is a terrible mistake. Do I enjoy telling these stories? No. It brings tears to my eyes every time. But it has to be done.

HOME

Some of Canada's most important contributions to the Allied war effort came from the home front. Canada donated more than three billion dollars to Britain during the course of the war, allowing the old country to keep buying munitions and food in Canada and the United States. The remarkably high Canadian output of war materiel—from ships and tanks to bombers and shells, as well as some eight hundred thousand trucks—was just the tip of the iceberg. The factories worked day and night to supply the Allied forces. The battle fronts could not have existed without the home fronts.

The British Commonwealth Air Training Program (BCATP) was one of Canada's most important contributions in support of our Allies. There had been pre-war discussions about organizing a Commonwealth-wide air-training program, but the idea had never really gotten off the ground. After Canada went to war, Prime Minister William Lyon Mackenzie King sought desperately to avoid the unlimited commitment of the Great War, which had

resulted in the grinding casualties of the Western Front that had ultimately led to the 1917 conscription crisis. After much wrangling over costs, Canada agreed to pay the lion's share of the enormous air-training program. That decision eventually resulted in the building of airstrips and schools across the country, and the training of more than 131,000 aircrew members, most from across the British Commonwealth but also the United States, France, and Poland. While this was a significant contribution towards winning the war, the savage nature of the air war did not allow for King's hope for a limited commitment. Some 17,101 Canadians were killed while serving in the air force.

At home, tens of thousands of Canadians were involved in protecting the nation from an invasion that never came. Coastal guns, air force squadrons, and a growing number of warships sought to protect merchant shipping from the hunting U-boats. Canada's vulnerability was revealed in the summer of 1942, when U-boats pushed down the St. Lawrence and sank a number of vessels, causing great alarm. Along the West Coast, the threat of Japanese naval attacks, and the shelling of an isolated lighthouse at Estevan Point on June 20, 1942, created far more fear in the press and amongst the public than these excursions deserved. A joint Canadian and American strike force planned to attack the Japanese in the Aleutian Islands in August 1943, but the enemy had retreated from the island of Kiska only weeks before to avoid the battle. There was a minor threat from nine thousand or so unmanned fire balloons that the Japanese launched against North America to set the wooded interior ablaze. The balloons were generally useless, although there was worry late in the war that the desperate Japanese might load them with biological agents. They never carried such lethal cargo, although Canadian scientists did manufacture all manner of chemical and biological agents, largely at Grosse Île, Quebec, and Suffield, Alberta. Many Canadian veterans became human guinea pigs as the chemicals were tested on them. Some suffered long-term damage.

To protect against the outward threat, Canadians also built up the interior. Canada worked with the United States to construct the Alaska Highway, which helped to protect the relatively undefended north from Japanese invasion by allowing for the more rapid movement of troops along interior lines. But this led to new concerns as the American engineers and labour formations seemed to be a quasi-occupying force.

Thousands of over-aged Canadians, many of them veterans of the Great War, served in uniform to protect strategic ports, buildings, and canals. They also guarded thirty-four thousand German prisoners of war, who began to filter into the country from the various battle fronts. Most of the prisoners were compliant, but there were hardcore Nazis in the ranks who often threatened, assaulted, and even murdered other prisoners, keeping up the fight for the Führer from behind barbed wire.

Supporting the fighting services and the training in England was a vast organizational apparatus to administer to the needs of hundreds of thousands of Canadians in uniform. Pay and benefits, death notices and pensions, file after file was needed to keep track of the forces in Canada and overseas. This paper war was not glamorous, but it was essential to run the armed forces, deal with claims of wounded wartime or postwar veterans, and provide mountains of evidence for future historians.

Corinne Kernan Sévigny

BORN » MONTREAL, QUEBEC
BRANCH » CANADIAN WOMEN'S ARMY CORPS (CWAC)
TRADE » RECRUITER
HOMETOWN » MONTREAL, QUEBEC

A Canadian Women's Army Corps recruiter in Quebec, Corinne Sévigny played a prominent role in the "extraordinary feminist revolution" that saw tens of thousands of women enlist during the Second World War.

It was 1941 and the CWAC had just been started. It was a totally new thing to have women in the army. I think we may have been 1,500 when I joined up. Then, all of a sudden, we were several thousand women, but at the beginning it wasn't something that was accepted. I can remember that my poor parents were often asked how they could let their only daughter join the army. Even my friends would say that I was completely crazy, that it was just something that wasn't done. For many of my friends it was simply inconceivable and unacceptable that a woman of my age could leave the house to join the army.

The idea that Quebec was not a part never entered our minds—we had many more important battles to fight—so it became imperative that we become first and foremost accepted as human beings. Most men were not convinced that we women were able to take on the task at hand, not even sure we were able to do the simplest of tasks. We had no choice other than to step up to the plate. We were the pioneers. We were the ones who could show them that women could take on any serious assignment such as the telegraph, the telephone, anything that was new and needed in the army. Throughout the development of the conflict, this huge war, there were many developments, technically speaking. There were many that were pioneered by women. You only have to look at the history books to see. I wanted to be a part of the group that would defend against what was happening around the world. It was without a doubt the most important thing happening at that time. If we weren't going to be a part of it, then we were home just twiddling our thumbs. Or, that was how I thought it was, but that might not necessarily be true; evidently so, because there were many women who were not standing idly by doing nothing during the war.

Women went to work in the factories. It was unheard of before then. Thousands of women went to work in the factories. It was an extraordinary feminist revolution!

Apart from being a maid, good dancer, nurse, telephone operator, servant, cook, do you know of any other things a woman could do before the war? Women were simply not holding any extraordinary, serious, or centrally complex jobs. It just wasn't done! We had the responsibility of proving that women could take on important responsibilities at any time. Today, it is common to see women at the helm of huge corporations. It wasn't conceivable [then] that a woman could be anything higher than a secretary. At the beginning, they thought we knew nothing. When we finished our courses—courses on vehicle maintenance, mechanical courses—we knew the difference between the wheels on the vehicle, and we were able to learn the decoding and coding, yes! We learned it all!

During the war, day-to-day life hadn't changed all that much, except for the women. At one point, we women came to be accepted just like everyone else.

"We had no choice other than to step up to the plate. We were the pioneers."

Top: A CWAC parade.
Centre: Sévigny and Captain Lucien Cote during a Victory Bonds campaign.
Bottom: Sévigny speaking over CKCV Radio, Quebec City.

Donald Stevenson

BORN » BRITISH COLUMBIA

BRANCH » TRAINING COMMAND,
ROYAL CANADIAN AIR FORCE

TRADE » PILOT

HOMETOWN » BRITISH COLUMBIA

Donald Stevenson joined the Royal Canadian Air Force in 1942, eager to go overseas and do his part for the war effort. A skilled pilot, he helped train thousands of other air force personnel from all over the world for the British Commonwealth Air Training Plan.

I was relegated to what was called Training Command; training others in aircrew trades to go overseas and fight our enemies. All of us who were stuck in the training end of things were anxious to get out of it and get overseas ourselves.

We all started at what was known as a manning depot, which is where you went for your basic training and your indoctrination. You got your uniforms and your inoculations and all the horrible things they did to us in those days. You were selected to be whatever aircrew trade they felt you were most suited for. I was selected for pilot training. When you got your pilot's wings, you were posted to whatever duties they had in line for you.

Essentially what we did was fly people around while they learned their trades. We weren't involved directly in the training of the younger men, we were simply performing a function so that their own instructors could teach them their trade. I wouldn't say that fellows that were chosen for staff jobs were any better or any worse than anybody else. They just happened to be available and the need was there and that was it. You didn't have any choice.

One of the great things was the opportunity of meeting young men from all over the world that came to Canada under the British Commonwealth Air Training Plan. We had boys from the Royal Air Force in Britain. And from the Rhodesian Air Force, from the South African Air Force. Some Free French. A lot of Americans. People from other countries who had escaped from Europe and gone to Britain were sent over here to train.

We had a vital job to do, but it wasn't what we'd hoped we were going to do. It wasn't exactly exciting. But as the old saying is, "A dirty job but somebody had to do it."

"I wouldn't say that fellows that were chosen for staff jobs were any better or any worse than anybody else. They just happened to be available."

Really there was a certain amount of excitement at times, a certain amount of risk. In early 1945, the Japanese started sending hydrogen balloons over to Canada with bombs hanging in baskets under them. Many of us were alerted to go out and shoot these things down. It so happened I was flying planes that had machine guns on them and we were alerted for that purpose. Those balloons did float across western Canada and the western U.S.A. and there were some civilians killed. When kids on a picnic found one of these baskets in the woods in Oregon, they went and got their teacher. And they disturbed the thing. The bombs exploded and six of them were killed.

That was about as close as we came to enemy activity. We were sworn to a special oath of secrecy, which didn't last very long, but at the time was pretty exciting.

Top left: On first leave at a railway station in Kingston, Ontario.
Bottom left: Stevenson is presented with his "wings," August 20, 1943.
Above: At bombing and gunnery school, Paulson, Manitoba, June 2, 1945.

Catherine Anderson

BORN » WINNIPEG, MANITOBA

BRANCH » ROYAL CANADIAN AIR FORCE,
WOMEN'S DIVISION

TRADE » ADMINISTRATIVE CLERK

HOMETOWN: NEW WESTMINSTER, BRITISH COLUMBIA

Like most military personnel, Catherine Anderson wished to serve her country overseas during the Second World War. Due to her age—seventeen, although she had told the recruiters she was eighteen—she was not given the chance. Following service in Nova Scotia, she was transferred to RCAF Headquarters in Ottawa to work in the casualty records branch.

My first posting when I graduated from training school was Halifax. I was supposed to be going overseas, but when I got there, this new rule came out that no woman could go overseas unless you were twenty-one. Some of the girls were going over there and they were getting pregnant and it wasn't acceptable. And I thought, "Well, my goodness, you can get pregnant in Canada just as well as you can overseas." Anyway, they wouldn't let me go, so I went to Cape Breton Island.

My first Christmas away from home, and here I was seventeen. I couldn't get home for Christmas, so I told the boss—he was a wonderful man, a sergeant—that I would stay, I would be the skeleton crew for Christmas at the office. He didn't want that. He said, no, there were two girls—sisters—that were in my barrack block. They lived in Halifax and they had invited me to their home for Christmas. One was Doris and the other was Claire, and their name was McAndrew. Sergeant Brown decided that I should go with them, so I did. And that Christmas was the most memorable one I've ever had. I didn't get a parcel from home, it came late, and I got there and everybody had a gift for me and the girls had a brother that was home for Christmas weekend.

We all went to church and it was just like a picture postcard. We walked to church from their house and it was up on a little hill. We came out of church and it was snowing. I could not believe this. It was coming down snowing, just like a Norman Rockwell thing. It was absolutely wonderful. And we walked home throwing snowballs and just had a wonderful Christmas. Their parents had an open

Anderson, summer 1943.

house all the time. They had a guestbook on the front table, everybody signed it and it was just like in the movies. It was wonderful.

It was when I was there that we got word that my brother, who was just a little bit older than me, had been killed in Italy. Mom asked if I could get a compassionate posting closer to home, so that's when I went to Ottawa.

I went to the records office there. It was a very boring job. It was keeping the records of all the people from the air force; all their tests, examinations and everything else would come to Ottawa and then we would transfer them into their card and file away. Everybody had a file. And then I went into the records office casualty branch. When we were on the day shift, we would be writing letters to the next of kin, informing them of whatever had happened to their loved ones, whether they were killed in action or missing in action or prisoner of war or something. It was so much harder for me. I had had my one brother that was killed and then my other brother, who

"We would be writing letters to the next of kin, informing them of whatever had happened to their loved ones, whether they were killed in action or missing in action or prisoner of war."

was in the tank corps, he went over on D-Day, which was June 6 [1944], and he was very, very badly wounded. And when you have that, and then you have to tell somebody else that these things have happened to their loved ones, it's a little hard.

When we were on the night shift, we were on the teletype and we received the wires that came in. We would get the airman's files so that the day shift would have them ready so they could write the letters. John Gillespie Magee was an American in our Canadian Air Force. He was killed, but he had written a poem called "High Flight." It was in one of the files that I had to retrieve one time when I was working. It's a beautiful poem.

The cast of a musical in which Anderson performed while in Sydney, Nova Scotia, 1943.

A fellow airwoman poses in her gas mask and helmet in Sydney, Nova Scotia, 1943.

A copy of "High Flight," in Magee's own handwriting. This copy was included in a letter he sent home to his parents. Courtesy of LAC.

High Flight

Oh! I have slipped the surly bonds of Earth
And danced the skies on laughter-silvered wings;
Sunward I've climbed, and joined the tumbling mirth
of sun-split clouds, - and done a hundred things
You have not dreamed of - wheeled and soared and swung
High in the sunlit silence. Hov'ring there,
I've chased the shouting wind along, and flung
My eager craft through footless halls of air ....

Up, up the long, delirious, burning blue
I've topped the wind-swept heights with easy grace
Where never lark, or even eagle flew -
And, while with silent, lifting mind I've trod
The high untrespassed sanctity of space,
- Put out my hand, and touched the face of God.

Robert "Tommy" Atkins

BORN » OAKVILLE, ONTARIO

BRANCH » THE LORNE SCOTS, CANADIAN ARMY

TRADE » PLATOON COMMANDER

HOMETOWN » KING CITY, ONTARIO

Robert "Tommy" Atkins served as a lieutenant with the Lorne Scots, the regiment that provided the headquarters defence units for the 13th Canadian Infantry Brigade. Following the Japanese occupation of Alaska's Aleutian Islands, Atkins took part in the August 1943 "joint exercise between the Americans and the Canadians" to retake the island of Kiska: the Japanese forces retreated before the Allies arrived.

We went out to the Aleutians in 1943. It was a joint exercise between the Americans and the Canadians. The Americans had a division and we had a brigade, so we were outnumbered about, oh, four to one. I think the Canadians had five thousand troops in that organization and the Americans had about twenty thousand. This was in the summertime and we were outfitted with winter gear in Nanaimo [British Columbia]. So we knew it was going to be a fairly cold operation, but we didn't know where it was at that time.

We got down to training and some of the troops were sent up to Courtenay, B.C., for a combined operation/landing operations training. I guess everybody was a little nervous. At that time, we weren't sure whether the Japs were there or not, because there had been no sightings of any Japanese from the air for about a week. We thought maybe they'd just gone to ground and were waiting for us to land.

"So we went ahead with the operation and when we landed, there were no Japanese anywhere."

It turned out that our commanding general figured that if the Japs were not there, it would be good training for us to go through with the landing anyway. And if they were, we'd have a scrap. So we went ahead with the operation and when we landed, there were no Japanese anywhere. The Americans suffered something like twenty dead in the operations and the Canadians suffered four—mostly

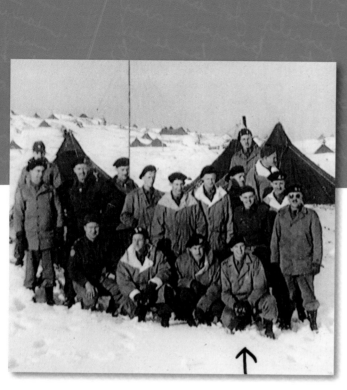

from mines, booby traps, and friendly fire. People were landing and they weren't sure if the people they saw in the fog were friends or foe, so sometimes they just shot to find out.

The weather was not very friendly. The Aleutian Islands are situated at a place in the ocean where the warm waters from the Japanese current come up on the south side of the chain of islands and the Siberian currents with the cold water come down the north side. So when the air masses over these waters collide, you get fog, rain, snow, etcetera. We were there until New Year's 1944. When we were landing in the Aleutian Islands, the Canadians [the 1st Canadian Infantry Division] were landing in Sicily.

Top left: Atkins (see the arrow) with HQ 13 Canadian Infantry Brigade in Kiska.
Bottom left: Diary of Defence Platoon (The Lorne Scots), 1943.
Above: Japanese Zero Fighter Manufacturer's Identity Panel, 1943.

Margarita "Madge" Trull

BORN » VALPARAÍSO, CHILE

BRANCH » WOMEN'S ROYAL NAVAL SERVICE
(WRNS, A.K.A.: WRENS)

TRADE » INTELLIGENCE WRITER

HOMETOWN » MISSISSAUGA, ONTARIO

Madge Trull joined the Women's Royal Naval Service (WRNS) in October 1943, after originally seeking to enlist as a nurse. While her discharge papers record her occupation as a "writer," she "didn't even know what to do as a secretary." Here she describes her work on the ULTRA secret, helping to decode German signal traffic.

I joined with my sister Jean Janes, or Jeannie, I called her. We both went to Portsmouth in England to join up in the Women's Royal Naval Service. I had wanted to be a nurse, but it was all filled up. But we got chosen for the WRNS, which was delightful because I liked the idea of the WRNS.

At Eastcote, we trained as cryptologists, or whatever it is they called us. We were only supposed to be known—very secretive work—as "writers." On my discharge papers, I was an "intelligence writer," and "writer" meant "secretary," and I had never been a secretary—didn't even know what to do as a secretary. Now, they call it the ULTRA secret.

After Eastcote, we were sent to Stanmore, where we were really decoding German messages. We worked in what were called "bays." And in those bays, there were these huge machines called "bombes." The bombes were sort of a mechanical apparatus, if you want to call it that. They were big. Very, very noisy. They had on them drums, and on these drums were tons of little wires. But if one wire crossed another wire, it would mess up the whole decoding system. So we had to be sure that they were all cleared out and running perfectly. It was kind of hard on our nervous system, even though we were pretty young.

When we had maybe broken a code—which the machine helped us to do, but we had to set it up—we then had to go into a little room with a machine that looked like the Enigma, and work it back. Now, we weren't able to read those codes. Those codes were sent to Bletchley Park by a courier. We didn't know much about it at the time, but I've learned that since.

We were sworn under the *Official Secrets Act*, which was for ninety years. I haven't reached that yet, but there are certain things that have to be kept quiet, and I'm never a hundred per cent sure what I can or what I can't talk about. At the time, if we had divulged anything, we could have either been sent up to detention camp, or—believe it or not—shot! We were very careful not to speak to anybody about it. My mother died not knowing what I did.

"We were very careful not to speak to anybody about it. My mother died not knowing what I did."

Above: In Bournemouth, England, October 1943.

Top right: Madge and friends at WRENS' quarters at Stanmore, Middlesex, England.

Bottom right: Husband John C. Trull, flight lieutenant in the RCAF, Madge and Jeannie in London, England.

Bottom left: Enigma machine.

Robert Rodgers

BORN » SOUTHAMPTON, ONTARIO

BRANCH » ROYAL CANADIAN AIR FORCE; CANADIAN ARMY

TRADE » PRISONER OF WAR CAMP GUARD

HOMETOWN » SOUTHAMPTON, ONTARIO

In 1942, Robert Rodgers gave up the "dust and noise and heat" of an Owen Sound steel foundry to enlist in the Royal Canadian Air Force (RCAF). One snafu after another—including being sent to Clinton, Ontario, rather than Clinton, England—convinced him to try the army instead. Rodgers served out the war as a guard at the camp for German prisoners in Farnham, Quebec.

They shipped us up to Arnprior, [near] Ottawa. And up there, we learned engines and mathematics. Then they decided that they were going to ship us overseas, so they told us one morning to get our packs ready. The trucks came to pick us up and take us on the train. We figured it was the train, anyway. They didn't tell us, they just told us where we were leaving.

So they had enough trucks until the last: there was eight of us still standing there and the truck, but no driver. About an hour later, they come up with their driver. It was black dark. They handed him the big envelope with our orders in it and said, "Away you go." So we got in the truck, all blanketed in this canvas, and we thought we were going down maybe a half hour's run to the railroad station. But we drove and we drove and we drove for an hour and a half, two hours. And we heard a gate open in front of us. We drove in, made a U-turn and the driver got out and said, "Alright, out you get." So we all jumped out in the middle of a parade square. And he handed us the envelope with all our orders, got in the truck and drove away.

There was nobody around; the lights were pretty well all out by this time. Some guy came walking along and said, "What are you fellows doing here?" "Well, they just brought us here." "Well," he said, "you can't be out in the light," he said. "Go up and get in that empty hut there, upstairs is open. Stay there until morning." So we did that. There was just mattresses on the bunks up there. We got up the next morning, went down to the mess hall and ate—for three days we ate and slept up there. Finally, an officer and two men walked in and asked what we were

Training Platoon, Newmarket, Ontario, 1945. Rodgers is the third from left, middle row.

doing there. We handed him the orders. "Yeah," he said, "This is Clinton. But you're supposed to be in Clinton, England, not Clinton, Ontario. The rest of your outfit's probably about two days out in the ocean in the boat."

So then they took us down to London [Ontario] and put us up. They told us that they didn't need any more flight engineers. They said we were all going back to being just ground crew. I said, "That's sweeping floors, isn't it?" And they said, "That's about it." I transferred over that day into the army.

They sent us to Newmarket for basic training, and when we finished there, I went down to Farnham, Quebec, for advanced [training]. It had a population I guess of about a thousand people. And there were five hotels in it. All you could buy was Dawes Black Horse ale in quarts. And they had no refrigeration.

They picked out a few of us to work at a German prisoner-of-war camp for German officers. In the morning, we'd take a prisoner by Jeep or small truck out to a farm.

The prisoners would either hoe potatoes or tomatoes or whatever the Frenchmen wanted them to do. And we'd have to guard him for the day. They'd come out and pick us up late in the afternoon and take us back into camp. I did that for about three weeks in the spring.

After that, we would stand on the towers or they'd send us out to surround the camp. They were very strict with the prisoners. We had to watch that they didn't break out. They wanted to get down into the United States, and we were only ninety miles from the border.

Twice they broke out when we were there. They went out over the fence. I was sleeping in the bunks when the sirens went and I had to get out and go, and by the time I got after them, they were fifteen or twenty miles south of the camp, across the railroad tracks. The sergeant spotted one of them going through the water. It was up to between this lad's knees and his waist. And he said, "Do you see'em?" I said, "Yeah." "Well," he said, "Don't stand there," he said, "shoot' em." I said, "You mean you want me to shoot them?" And he said, "That's what we're here for." So that was the only time I ever shot a rifle at a man. We got both of them that time. He was standing there giving me orders, in fact, he had to give it to me twice before I did it. That's the only time I used the old .303 Lee-Enfield on a man.

Top: War Medal (1939–45).
Bottom: Flight 75, Pre-air Training School, Toronto, Ontario, 1944. Rodgers is the third from left, middle row.

"I was sleeping in the bunks when the sirens went and I had to get out and go, and by the time I got after them, they were fifteen or twenty miles south of the camp, across the railroad tracks."

Marcel Caron

BORN » MONTREAL, QUEBEC

BRANCH » THE ROYAL CANADIAN POSTAL CORPS, CANADIAN ARMY

TRADE » POSTMAN

HOMETOWN » MONTREAL, QUEBEC

A conscript, Marcel Caron spent his service on the home front with the Royal Canadian Postal Corps. His duties involved sorting and distributing mail for soldiers overseas and German prisoners of war in Canada.

They decided to start calling up people as they turned twenty-one, to complete a three-month period [of service]. I turned twenty-one on January 23, 1941, and the day after my birthday, I received a letter from the federal government. Monsignor Devoir, my family doctor, was to give me a physical exam that he would refer to the government. A couple of weeks later, I received a letter from the army telling me to attend the basic training camp in Saint-Jerôme.

The army held a recruiting drive because they needed candidates for the [Royal Canadian] Postal Corps. They had their base post office in Ottawa. There, they received all of the mail from all the soldiers who were overseas and all of the soldiers in Canada at the big outposts like Valcartier,

Borden, Petawawa, even the air force. I was transferred to Valcartier. There was only one sergeant, one corporal and two privates. I was one of the privates.

We would meet the train from Chicoutimi and other places at around two or three in the morning. During the day, we would go to Quebec City, to the post office that had all of the mail for Valcartier. There were a lot of packages for soldiers who were overseas. It all had to go through Valcartier. After getting the mail we would go into each hut to distribute it. One day, I was in a hut and I started yelling out names, "Mr. So-and-So, Mr. So-and-So." I came across a name, let's say it was Gustave So-and-So, and I gave him his letter. The guys around him all said, "You got a letter? Who wrote you?" So he opened the envelope. He had received five sheets with nothing written on them, and on the last page all that was written was a signature. So people started asking him, "You call that a letter?" The guy, he said, "Yes, but it's from my brother and we haven't spoken in five years." When we would distribute the mail,

"When we would distribute the mail, everyone would come to see if there was something for them. It was so important for a soldier's morale."

At the military base in Kingston, Ontario, 1941.

everyone would come to see if there was something for them. It was so important for a soldier's morale.

It was so important that the tobacco companies started a promotion: for one dollar, you could buy three hundred cigarettes; for three dollars, you could buy a thousand cigarettes. People would send money to Imperial Tobacco or Macdonald and then the company would send a card to the soldier overseas. The postal corps had a tobacco depot so that the soldier who was overseas could pick up his cigarettes.

We were also looking after the Germans soldiers who were here. At the beginning of the war, the prisoners that were captured were brought to Canada. They were in different places: on Sainte-Hélène's Island or in Hull. The parents of those prisoners would send them mail. The postal corps had the entire list of prisoners and where they were located. You would be surprised how well the people in Germany took care of the prisoners that were here.

Nellie Rettenbacher

BORN » NICKEL VALLEY, BRITISH COLUMBIA
BRANCH » CANADIAN WOMEN'S ARMY CORPS
TRADE » MILITARY POLICEWOMAN
HOMETOWN » MERRITT, BRITISH COLUMBIA

A Métis from the British Columbia interior, Nellie Retten-bacher was not content with serving in a "traditional" role with the Canadian Women's Army Corps (CWAC). After completing basic training, she became a military police-woman.

In June 1943, I enlisted in the Canadian Army in Van-couver, and I stayed in until July 1946. I took my basic training in Vermillion, Alberta, in July of 1943 and from there, I was sent to Gordon Head, an officers' training cen-tre near Victoria, B.C. Then I went to a workforce barracks in Victoria, B.C., for a short while. Then they opened up a place in Chilliwack, B.C., at Vedder Crossing army base. They needed staff. About sixty of us girls were the first group to go.

We were put in the officers' quarters because they didn't have the quarters for us ready yet. It was a big army camp and we had a lot of fun there. Then, all of a sud-den, I thought, I don't want to do this work around the kitchen, so I asked if I could join the military police. And my officer said, "Sure, I'll put you on." So they sent me to military police training in Camp Borden, Ontario. From there, I was sent back to Vancouver, and spent the rest of the time there on patrol. I was promoted to corporal, and I had about three or four girls working for me, which was a pretty good life. I really enjoyed the military.

I was what they call a "half breed." There were quite a few Indian girls in the army. I was not raised on a reserve, and I didn't go to Indian schools like a lot of the other girls did. I never had any problem with that in the army whatso-ever. They treated me equally and I treated them the same.

We would go down to the train station or bus depots and see the girls coming and going. We just made sure they had their passes with them. We would make sure that they were back to barracks on time—they had to be in by 2400 hours. Of course, some of the girls would get into a bit of a mischief, and we had to see that they would behave themselves. If they were with their boyfriends, army guys,

"I thought, I don't want to do this work around the kitchen, so I asked if I could join the military police."

they would get a little bit mouthy with us. But the male MPs [military police] were always nearby. So if we needed their help, we could just call them and that was it.

At times, I would be working at the barracks, at the office there. We had to have the lights out at a certain time, but the girls would come home after a party and they'd go upstairs and turn all the lights on. I would have to go up and ask them to turn the lights off. And they would usually tell me where to go and what to do. So I would get some of the girls that were working with me, and we would call one of the officers and get them straightened around a bit. We never had to do anything physical with them. They knew they would be into trouble if we did—confined to barracks for a week. I found that talking to them quietly was better than telling them who is boss—that I was a corporal and they were just a private. It all worked out.

Top: CWAC soldiers, August 1, 1942. Rettenbacher is in the top row, second from the left.
Bottom: CWACs on parade in England.

Mike Hawryliw

BORN » FENWOOD, SASKATCHEWAN

DECEASED » SASKATOON, SASKATCHEWAN (2009)

BRANCH » CANADIAN ARMY

TRADE » TANK DRIVER

HOMETOWN » SASKATOON, SASKATCHEWAN

Mike Hawryliw saw action in Northwest Europe during the Second World War, but he remembers his service in Canada much more vividly, thanks to the time he spent at the Experimental Station Suffield in southern Alberta. Hawryliw was one of the hundreds of military volunteers subjected to chemical weapons tests at the site during the war. Sworn to secrecy, he did not even tell his family about the experiments until fifty years later.

When this Suffield [Experimental Station] thing came up, I wanted to know more. I was waiting to go to training and it wasn't coming. One morning, the officer asked for volunteers to go for this gas experiment. Somebody said, "Is it dangerous?" "Well," he said, "yes, but they usually come back in good shape." So I said okay. There were fifteen of us who volunteered to go in that group.

They were fair about it: they told us just before departure that we could back out. There would be no money involved other than our $1.30 a day army pay, but we would get two days for every week we were there. As a result, I got ten days leave and two days travelling time. They asked that, when we walked out of the gates, we say nothing to anyone about what happened or what we'd seen. We were to keep it a secret. I took this seriously. I never told my family. I don't know if some of the others did or not, that was their business.

We were thirty or fifty miles out of Medicine Hat [Alberta], in the hills. All there was was brush and tall grass. It was very enclosed, to keep the public out. In the regular army camps, at breakfast time, you got a little bit of porridge and coffee. But at Suffield, you sat at the table and had packaged cereals, tea, coffee or milk—real food. Boy, isn't this nice, eh? And somebody else would pipe up and say, "Yeah, they're feeding you good because tomorrow we might not be here." But they treated us good.

They'd put dabs of gas on your arm through the thickness of your uniform. And then they said, "Go to bed. This is going to itch, but don't scratch it." By morning,

"They asked that, when we walked out of the gates, we say nothing to anyone about what happened or what we'd seen. We were to keep it a secret."

there was a blister there, big as a fifty-cent piece. So we had to report to the hospital. The experiment was not only to create a blister, but how to treat it. They had a lab there that perfected ointments.

In time, the blister went down, but for years, there was a little mark where the blister had been. And then there were other experiments. They would have a gas shell blow and we would be standing there with our masks on, with a rabbit in a cage, facing one way, and a goat in the pit facing the other way. You could hear the shell going ahead and the wind would blow the vapour. We heard that some of the animals died on the way back to camp because they had no masks, but we did. That was good to know, because in the future, I would have to depend on that mask.

Later, we did get twenty-four thousand dollars. Got a letter and in it was a cheque for twenty-four thousand dollars for the service at Suffield. And since then, the DVA [Department of Veterans Affairs] has put out a notice because some of the participants in Suffield didn't tell their families that they had been there. What the DVA wanted was for the families of veterans who had been at Suffield to be eligible for that twenty-four thousand dollars. If you know someone, tell them to go to DVA.

Sometime after the war, I was sitting at the Legion around the beer table and some of the guys were talking. One guy had a leg off and another guy had this, another guy had that. And one guy piped up and said, "I was in Suffield under those gas experiments." And the other guys looked at him and they said, "Ah, you're full of it, you know. You're just saying that." After that, I kept my mouth shut.

Department of National Defence Certificate of Appreciation presented to Hawryliw in 2003, along with twenty-four thousand dollars compensation. Hawryliw in uniform with armoured corps beret at age twenty, circa 1942.

Gordon Hardy

BORN » INGONISH, NOVA SCOTIA

BRANCH » SS LORD STRATHCONA AND SS ROSE CASTLE, CANADIAN MERCHANT NAVY

TRADE » MESS STEWARD

HOMETOWN » INGONISH, NOVA SCOTIA

A steward on the SS *Rose Castle* when it was torpedoed off Newfoundland by the German submarine *U-518* on November 2, 1942, Cape Breton–native Gordon Hardy managed to survive exposure in the North Atlantic—thanks in part to the assistance of a relative he did not even know he had.

I joined the merchant navy when I was seventeen in 1941. We sailed from Sydney, Nova Scotia to iron ore mines in Bell Island [Newfoundland]. On November 2 [1942], we were loaded [aboard the SS *Rose Castle*] and anchored off Conception Bay [Newfoundland], waiting to go to Sydney. Some time after midnight, I heard an awful explosion. I jumped out of bed. There was a light over my bed, with a chain, and I pulled it. There was no light, so I knew we were torpedoed.

I ran out on deck with my life jacket in my hand, or so I thought. When I got on deck, there was the third engineer and the second engineer and they had a flashlight. I saw that I had my pillow with me instead of my life jacket! I always slept with my lifebelt under my pillow. I threw down the pillow and ran and got my life jacket.

I ran to the railing and they said, "Where are you going, Hardy?" I said, "I'm going over the side." They said, "Don't jump in that cold water, it'll kill you." I said it was better to jump in the cold water and take a chance on that than to be killed by another torpedo. They asked if I thought we were going to get another one. And I said, "We'll get it any second now. We'll get two." I went headfirst. Just as I struck the water, they say, the torpedo struck on the opposite side through the engine room. She went down in fifty seconds.

The suction took me down with her. But I was swimming all the time. When I came back up, I swam and swam. I had taken in water and that slowed me down, made me half sick, and I was starting to get cold then because there were snow flurries and cold wind. I could hear people calling to God and the Virgin Mary around me in the dark. Everything was dark, pitch dark.

Father & Five Sons In Services

Five sons of Mr. and Mrs. Levi Hardy, of North Bay, Ingonish, are serving their country in various branches of the services. Shown above are Claude, who lost his life at sea as a member of the Merchant Marine, Gordon, who is stationed at Aldershot, Harold at Yarmouth, Wilfred in England, and William in Italy.

I was in the water at least a couple of hours. I came across a life raft, and this fellow reached out his hand. I was too weak then, too cold, to pile on the raft, so he reached his hand out and he said, "I'm very pleased to meet you, Gordon." He said, "We're first cousins." That's the first time I had ever seen him or heard tell of him. He was from Port Aux Basques, Newfoundland, and he had a brother onboard. His brother went down in the ship that night, and he survived. He pulled me in and I had no clothes on. I was so cold that I had to get back down in the water. There was a hole in the centre of the raft with a bottom to it. I had to stand down in that because it was warmer in the water.

A Fairmile [D-motor torpedo boat] came alongside and picked us up off of the raft. I couldn't stand so one fellow reached down and the other fellow held him. And he locked both hands on my wrists. And that was the greatest feeling that I ever felt. I knew I was going to make it.

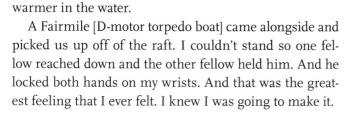

Above: Newspaper clipping noting how the Hardy family (father and five sons) were all serving in the war.
Left: The SS *Rose Castle*, on which Hardy sailed, September 11, 1942. She was torpedoed and sunk along with the *PLM 27* on November 2, 1942. Courtesy of LAC.

Margaret Plante

BORN » PEACE RIVER, ALBERTA

BRANCH » ROYAL CANADIAN AIR FORCE,
WOMEN'S DIVISION

TRADE » TIMEKEEPER/TYPIST

HOMETOWN » GRANDE PRAIRIE, ALBERTA

Margaret Plante first experienced city life after her enlistment in the Royal Canadian Air Force, Women's Division. Her service took her to different locales in Ontario and Quebec, but she opted not to go overseas.

I went from Edmonton to Rockcliffe, Ontario, for basic training. There were a lot of girls on that train that night we left Edmonton. I was all alone, not knowing anybody. I'd never even seen a city. I got terribly melancholy looking at the prairies. There was not a tree, and the sun was setting, and it was getting close to winter. I said, "What have I got myself into and where am I going?" I was so lonesome that I sat there and cried.

They gave me a posting to No. 3 Flying Instructor School in Arnprior, Ontario. I didn't know from Adam where that was. I went to the admin building the next morning to see the WD [Women's Division] officer. She said, "Tomorrow morning at 0800 hours, you report to Flight "D" as a timekeeper." I said, "What's that?" She said it was chalking up the flying officers' and pilots' time. I was working in the hangars. There were all these men sitting there. I was so embarrassed. I was so shy and backwards, from way back in the bush! I looked at them, and they start whistling at me. That was even worse.

In February 1944, I was posted overseas. The girls didn't have to go over if they didn't want to. I went to the WD officer and told her I didn't want to go because my brother was over there. He was with the 1st Canadian Division, and he went over in 1939 with the Loyal Edmonton Regiment. He told me they were bombing the heck out of England. "You stay in Canada," he said. "Don't come over here. It's dangerous to come over the waters—lots of U-boats [German submarines]." The WD said it was alright, that there would be other girls. And there were. But I kind of regretted it, after it was all over. I could have seen my brother, because he never came home. He was killed in the Italian campaign on December 14, 1944.

We were all posted to Lachine, Quebec. There was a

Plante outside the CWAC recruiting office in Ottawa, Ontario, 1944.

lot of typing to be done there: rows and rows and rows of paper, of names of men that were coming back from overseas to be discharged. There were numbers and rank and name and how much money they had coming. The first ones we did were about 1,500 prisoners of war that came back. They spent their whole doggone years in the air force as prisoners of war, shot down over enemy territory and other places. We went and met those boys when they came into the drill hall. They were in disarray, a lot of them. They'd just gotten out of the hospitals in England and they hadn't heard the latest tunes and they hadn't been eating very well. We bombarded them with a lot of hors d'oeuvres and fancy foods. And then our commanding officer gave them all cases of free beer. They weren't used to it, and some of them got very sick.

They didn't do that with the other batches of prisoners that came in. They just gave them ordinary sandwiches, nothing fancy. I was handing food to one of these fellows and he grabbed the whole tray and he just sat down there

"Car horns were blowing, people were running up and down the street. It was just like a zoo. My girlfriend said, 'Oh, the war is over!'"

and cried. He cried and cried and cried. I'd say he was maybe twenty-five or twenty-six years old. There was definitely something wrong with him. We had some orderlies from the medical corps there, so I got one of them. I said, "This fellow over here is in very, very bad shape." They went over and they took him out of the drill hall and to a hospital, I guess.

In May 1945, my girlfriend and I went to see this movie, *Rhapsody in Blue*. When we came out of that show—it was a matinee—there were papers flying all over. Car horns were blowing, people were running up and down the street. It was just like a zoo. My girlfriend said, "Oh, the war is over!" We were ten miles from Lachine, and we had to take a bus to get back to our station. But we couldn't get the buses—cars were stalled, everything was stalled. Someone grabbed my hat, and then someone else cut my girlfriend's tie. I said, "We'd better get out of here, or they're going to take our uniforms!"

That night, the commanding officer had a great big victory dance. I had a little black dress with little puffed sleeves and it had a gold belt at the waistline. And I had about two-and-a-half-inch-heel pumps to wear with that. And we had nylons. They were so sheer and you had to have that seam straight. So I had the nylons and a set of artificial pearls. Oh, we had a good time. That was the best dance I ever went to. The war was over.

Opposite, clockwise: Plante at the RCAF Women's Division barracks in Arnprior, Ontario, 1943; Plante (left) with fellow RCAF WD Sheila Huddleston at Lachine, Quebec, circa 1945–46; Before enlistment; Plante and RCAF (WD) comrades, circa 1944–45.

Above: A "Voices of Victory" voice recording that Margaret sent to her mother in April 30. These records could be played on any phonograph and carried greetings from Canadian service personnel to loved ones at home.

letter. I felt ever so sorry for my folks who would immediately receive a "missing" cable and then worry until the next one arrived. But leh will "cut no figure." Naturally can't tell you events or circumstances concerning recent experience but might say "It was a very hard fight Pop, but I won." Ended up finally slightly the worse for wear looking like a poplar tree in wintertime, weight 135 lbs. Not much meat on a frame like mine. But funny part was the fine teeth I show, going to leave it til I get to Cal. then get a good hairdresser & say "the works kid." Leaving for Calcutta tomorrow for a Medical Board & sick leave. Sorry Skirt, had to break off and dash away. There I go in Cal. Was quite sick at Tummy for a few days but

CONCLUSION

STORIES TOLD

In the Second World War—as in all wars of the past, present, and foreseeable future—it was ordinary men and women who were called upon to serve, fight, and sacrifice. For many years, however, the stories of their war efforts were relegated to personal memory.

The first and second generation of historians were drawn more readily to the generals and the movement of armies; to the strategic plans or evolving weapon systems; to the vast aerial or naval armadas; all of this and more, but rarely to the experience of those who served and fought. Nations struggled for their very survival. Entire populations supported the fighting forces and were willing to make nearly any sacrifice in the name of victory. This technological conflict, which saw incredible advances in armoured warfare, long-range bombers, fighter jets, aircraft carriers, U-boats, and unmanned rockets, all buttressed by the scientists who discovered or augmented radar, sonar, and navigational systems, seemed to suggest an impersonal war of faceless legions, except for some of the more identifiable commanders and politicians. But it goes without saying, although often without recording, that the largest armies, multi-ship convoys, and thousand-bomber raids all consisted of soldiers, sailors, and airmen. How these men and women endured the cold and misery, the fear and exhaustion, the strain and loss was the difference between victory and defeat.

This is a book that reminds us sharply of the human experience in the Canadian war effort, in all its multitudes, nuances, and complexities. There was no single war. No one could possibly see or understand all of the war's global components, campaigns, and theatres of battle. Yet through the millions of eye witnesses, we can glimpse aspects of this world war. Some of the history has been lost forever, disappearing with those who were buried in battle or behind the lines. But comrades lived on, and their stories of heroism and sacrifice were not forgotten. The traces, fragments, and shards of memory provide us with pieces to this puzzle of the past.

Service and sacrifice are watchwords for those who fought in the Second World War. As soon as a young man or woman entered the military forces, they were subject to new rules and realities, and cut off from their old lives. The things that mattered to these young Canadians as civilians might still have had an impact—like the popular songs of the day or mixing with the opposite sex—but there were new concerns. Many of the carefree delights of past lives were necessarily sacrificed as the young were forced into new areas of responsibility.

It is they who have sacrificed; it is we who have benefited. It is we who owe a debt to what many commentators have called the "greatest generation." Sons and daughters, aunts and uncles, fathers and friends served in uniform. Some forty-seven thousand remained overseas, forever, under Commonwealth War Graves Commission head stones. The survivors are now grandfathers, great aunts, or elderly parents. They have important stories to tell. It is our duty to listen, and to remember. TIM COOK

ABOUT THE MEMORY PROJECT

The Memory Project: Stories of the Second World War is a nationwide bilingual initiative that provides every living Second World War veteran in Canada with the opportunity to share his or her memories through oral interviews and digitized artifacts and memorabilia displayed on the website www.thememoryproject.com.

The Memory Project: Stories of the Second World War is a venture of The Historica-Dominion Institute (www.historica-dominion.ca), the largest charitable organization dedicated to history and citizenship in Canada. It is made possible by a contribution from the Government of Canada through the Celebrations and Commemorations Program of the Department of Canadian Heritage.

The project grew out of the success of The Memory Project Speakers' Bureau, which has enabled veterans to share their stories with more than a million students—directly in their classrooms—since its creation in 2001.

The sixty-five veteran profiles that comprise this book represent only a part of the project. In the first twelve months of the initiative, researchers conducted more than 1,400 interviews and collected nearly 7,000 artifacts. Currently, hundreds of interviews and thousands of artifacts are available at www.thememoryproject.com, where each of these veterans may also be heard telling his or her own story in his or her own voice. Interviews will continue until March 2011.

The interviewing process encouraged veterans to share their personal view of the monumental 1939–45 conflict. A pre-interview ensured that the project's staff gathered the same store of information for all of the veterans who shared their stories, including hometown, branch of service, and rank. This format further fostered the breakdown of potential barriers such as age differences and lack of familiarity between the interviewer and interviewee. The interviews themselves took place at special events—held in every province and in the Yukon—and veterans who were unable to attend an event participated by recording their stories over the telephone and couriering their memorabilia to the project's national office. Whatever the format, the interviewer and interviewee sat down one-on-one and veterans were always invited to speak on whatever subjects happened to be of most interest to them. The mixed format of in-person and telephone interviews helped the project reach the widest possible number of Second World War veterans.

Throughout, The Memory Project focused on the diversity of the Canadian experience, ensuring that various branches of service, ethnic and religious backgrounds, languages, military occupations, regions, and social classes were represented. Participants included not only veterans of the Canadian services, but also those who are now Canadian citizens, regardless of their nationality during the conflict.

The first-hand accounts in this book speak to fascinating yet often neglected issues, such as the importance of good cooks to warship morale, the role played by the rear gunner in a bomber flying low over Berlin, the vagaries of wartime romance, and the visceral consequences of battle exhaustion.

We Were Freedom: Canadian Stories of the Second World War serves the central purpose of the Memory Project: to create a legacy for posterity.

ANDREW THEOBALD
Ph.D., Research and Collections Officer,
The Memory Project: Stories of the Second World War

ACKNOWLEDGEMENTS

The publication of this book would not have been possible without the participation of the veterans featured within these pages, along with all of the veterans who have shared their stories with The Memory Project: Stories of the Second World War. These veterans agreed to serve their country once again—this time, it was not with blood and sweat, but with their wisdom and memories.

We wish to thank the programming team at the Department of Canadian Heritage, Celebrations and Commemorations, which generously supports the Project and was integral to its success.

The book was skilfully edited by Linda Pruessen of Key Porter Books and designed by Sonya V. Thursby, both of whom brought their enthusiasm and talent to these pages.

We are grateful to Tim Cook for lending his expertise and love of Canadian military history to the introduction and conclusion of this volume.

The Memory Project: Stories of the Second World War came to be through the passion and dedication of two people who envisioned the means for an entire generation of veterans to have their stories recorded for posterity—Marc Chalifoux and Jeremy Diamond.

The Project's successes would not have been possible without a team of dedicated interviewers, researchers, archivists, editors, transcribers, translators, web developers, and administrators who have spent the last year conducting thousands of interviews with veterans all across Canada.

Jenna Zuschlag Misener worked tirelessly as Project Manager of this ambitious undertaking. We would like to thank Jill Paterson, Shayla Howell, Jennifer Givogue, Sam Gojanovich, Stephanie Markowitz, Frances Cation, Marie-Eve Vaillancourt Deleris, Céline Garbay, Anne Seignot, Ric Pettit, Davida Aronovitch, Kathryn Stephens, Marc Pitre, Nichola Lobach, Alexia Yates, David Harkness, Judy Lam Maxwell, Eliana Tizel, Kailee Novikoff, Amy Robichaud-Harpe, Finlay Braithwaite, Wendy Neuhof, Anne Forrest-Wilson, Michel Beauchamp, Anne-Lise

226 Diehl, Ryan Catherine Breithaupt, Lucie Johanis, and the entire team at The Historica-Dominion Institute.

We would also like to thank James Marsh and Laura Bonikowsky at The Canadian Encyclopaedia for their support from the early days of the Project.

From the beginning, the Project relied on a group of advisors who offered support, guidance, and expertise in all areas of the organization. We would like to thank Dr. Jonathan Vance, Dr. Steven High, Dr. Jack Granatstein, Lt. Cdr (Ret'd) Albert Wong, Cdr Paul Seguna, Élizabeth Allard, Lt. Cdr (Ret'd) Howe Lee, Murray Brewster, Dr. Ronald Pruessen, Dr. James Woods, Richard Blackwolf, Zane Pieckenbrock, Shawna Ardley, Dr. Marco Fiola, Ted Barris, Sally Fur, Catherine Clement, Dr. Ellen Scheinberg, Cdr (Ret'd) William Gard, Mélodie Lachance, Dr. David Zimmerman, Chris Hughes, and J.D.M. Stewart.

Bill Maxwell and Royal Canadian Legion branches all across Canada answered our call for help in reaching veterans from coast to coast to coast—we would not have experienced such success without the work of their tireless staff and volunteers.

We would also like to thank K9 Design Co. and ecentricarts inc. for their work in bringing the Project to life visually and on the World Wide Web.

Finally, we would like to give a special thanks to Dr. Andrew Theobald, our in-house editor, who worked meticulously to ensure that this collection of stories would be representative of both the Project and Canada's participation in the Second World War.

NAME INDEX